Together Career make

JOSH DOUGLAS

[Together Career make]

The intertwining of professional careers and Family in academic partnerships.

Contents

1. "Linked Lives" in Science – Challenges for professional careersand coordination arrangements

The subject of this book is relationships within and outside of partnership factors the the professional careers from Women and men influence, if they live in an academic partnership. These are partnerships in those both partner above a academic degree and with it above a have very high potential for professional careers. Diverse sub- searches to professional careers from Women and academics show, that the increased educational resources and professional experiences of Women frequently not in professional careers and up with it couple level not be converted into dual careers. Such is the proportion of so-called Single-earner couples, in which only the man is employed, with academic partnerships have fallen from 44% (1971) to 17% (2004) (cf. Solga/ Rusconi 2008). nevertheless lay also 2004 the Portion at academic couples, in which both pursued a full-time professional activity, only at 30% In many this partnerships has itself therewith the professional role the Women changes, ie she go today majority an employment after. However, this often happens on a part-time basis and not always accordingly their level of education. Despite the considerable training investments of both partner has the plural the academic partnerships no dual career arrangement.

Why is it so difficult to achieve dual careers? And why do they still mostly fail because of the woman's career? In this A book want we Answer on this Ask give and us included in particular with the professional careers of women and men in science occupy. The basic assumption of our analyzes is that dual careers are the result of internal and external factors that are not each other act, rather in one reciprocal Relationship to each otherstand. This means that the institutions of the labor market jointly determine the career logic and professional cultures of scientific disciplines and the intra-partner coordination arrangements, to what extent the rhythms the career paths the both partner hierarchical or no matter

JOSH DOUGLAS

tär be reconciled (can be) and whether the respective professional success of both Partners (un)equal is (see section 1.3).

The data basis of the book is the collection of over 1,300 standard ated life course interviews with scientists from differentGerman colleges as well as from 45 theme-centric qualitative Interviews (see section 1.4). These interviews and their analysis took place in As part of the project "Make a career together. The intertwining of professional careers and Family in academic partnerships" at the Knowledge- Social Research Center Berlin (funded by the BMBF and the European Social Fund, see Foreword in this A book).

The subject of this chapter is, firstly, our analyzes of the career field Science as well as the historical Development from careers in the Embed pair context (see Sections 1.1 and 1.2). After that comments on the analytical framework and the central questions positions of the book (Section 1.3), on the data basis (Section 1.4.) as well as the definition of dual careers as used in the book (Section 1.5). Finally, important results of the subsequent the chapters with regard to the central question of the book after the obstacles for and realization conditions from dual careers in Academic partnerships accounted for (Section 1.6).

1.1 Women in science

The oldest university in Europe is the Law School of Bologna 1088 With it look European colleges on one above 900 year old History back - a history, however, from which women to the last ten years were persistently excluded. In the US, women were first admitted to college in 1833. In Europe it took reitern" France and Switzerland until 1865. And in Germany became women even not until 1908 the Access to study in everyone countries of German Reichs permitted (Geenen 1994: 23f.). However, until 1920 they were allowed to not habilitate (Mertens 1989: 5). Professional careers of women in of science on a larger scale are thus a relatively young phenomenon men.

The increase in the proportion of women among students in Germany up to to today's parity of about 50% was a lengthy process. until At the beginning of the Third Reich, the proportion of women among students increased next relatively quickly to 19% (1932). With the strongly traditional gender After the ideology of National Socialism, the proportion of women increased again 15% (1939) (Mertens 1989: 3). Only 1950 was in the two parts of so shared of Germany the level the Weimar republic again

"Linked Lives" in Science

reached. Since the 1960s, the economic miracle and the beginning educational expansion, the proportion of women steadily increases, albeit with different speeds in the GDR and the FRG. While it gender equality in the GDR as early as the mid-1970s when it came to studying (Geißler 1996: 278), this lasted in the Federal Republic of Germany or in reunified Germany until the transition into the 21st century. The degradation from inequalities at the general Access for the Studies between young men and women took almost a year hundred.

Between the subjects gives it size differences

regarding of historyof this development as well as in the proportion of women achieved today. So studied already in the Weimar Republic women above all medicine and philosophical cal subjects. In the Third Reich, the aforementioned decrease in women's share no way evenly above all subjects distributed. given of Contrary- between ideological beliefs and economic interests Since then, the proportion of women in medicine and pharmacy has increased; especially in the philosophical subjects as well as the law Sciences sank he however(cf. Mertens 1989).

This *horizontal segregation* in the fields of study of women and men puts itself until today away. So lies for example today the proportion of womenamong the first-year students of human medicine and the language and cultural studies at 66% and 74% respectively, in mathematics and the natural sciences at 41% and in engineering at 22% (please refer Illustration 1.1). Responsible for this are not more formal access restrictions, but socialization processes, gender ideologies and professional culture gender stereotypes as well as job-specific Career- opportunities for women (cf. Solga/Pfahl 2009).

Across the disciplines, however, the proportion of women from the Doctorate decreases with each career level, ie women to a greater extent as even educated Men the scientific career leave (must) (see Figure 1.1). Compared to the 1990s are here though some improvements to be noted, however, is particularly evident in the professorships – especially at the highest level (the C4 or W3 pro- fessuren) – a further sharp drop in the proportion of women compared to those with a doctorate, junior professorship or habilitation. The comparison of Appointments to C4 and W3 professorships (appointed since 2005) indicate shows a slight upward trend; The same applies to the comparison of the en proportion of junior professorships and habilitations. Given the Generational change and the associated increased possibility of new appointments to professorships in the last ten years, this company However, the difference or increase can be assessed as relatively small. after ending of alternation of generations (ie away approx. 2016) become – without ver- equal college expansion How End the 1960s and to beginning the *JOSH DOUGLAS* 1970s - significantly fewer professorships were filled, so that the women's share (excluding "quota" or other effective equal opportunities efforts) will then move even more slowly upwards, if he is under the Conditions of such a shortage of jobs and increased competition at all will continue to rise.

Figure 1.1: Percentage of women in different stages of a scientificlien Career, 2009/2010 (in %)

Source: statistical federal office (2009a: Tab. 4; 2009b: Tab. 3, 12; 2010: Tab. 7)

The synopsis of these findings shows that the disproportionate lust of women in the different transitions of a scientific chen career is present in all subject groups. He finds not only in the masculine dominated disciplines How the engineering or Natural sciences take place, but also in the mixed disciplines of Social sciences, law and economics and even in the female dominated disciplines such as linguistics and cultural studies or human medicine. Increasing or even equal proportions of women in the study Thus, graduates and trainees do not automatically bring increasing or equal opportunities for women at further academic career levels with himself. With the study of women, equality in the academic labor market – and, as we shall see (see Chapters 3 and 4 in this sem A book), in family work - not inevitably given.

"Linked Lives" in Science

Certainly, the university not only trains for science, and not all women and men study and do a doctorate with the professional goal science or professorship. Nevertheless, the question arises why Significantly fewer women than men take this career path or in remain in science and (can) achieve top positions there. This question arises all the more as the career opportunities outside of the Science not absolutely one attractive alternative for Women represent. On the contrary, it is also evident there that women do not use their qualifications in the same Scope How Men in professional careers and leading position can implement (cf. Holst 2009; Holst/Wiemer 2010). And even if it is assumed that some women do not *want both* - neither a car work in science or in business or administration – it stays that way the question still remains why not, when they are in education (in some cases up to a doctorate) have invested as much and for as long as Men. This book addresses these and other questions (see Section 1.3).

However, for answering this question, it is important not only that Requirements and obstacles in the professional field the Science to regard, but also the life and household context of women. Only one embedding from career requirements, professional decisions and Career paths in the couple context can be a question of ability and will as well as the barriers and realization conditions of scientific Careers of women - compared to men - adequately answered become (see section 1.3).

1.2 *Requirements for scientific careers in the double pack*

As mentioned earlier, historically women are a relatively new Appearance" at German universities. But although the proportion of women among the students strong increased is, was and is the Science given of low proportion of women on professorships always still one Institution, the from men shaped becomes and whose career paths traditional gender mus subject to the professional and private division of labor (Geenen 1994: 23). Academic careers and their requirements in the form of guidelines changes, work cultures, time structures as well as age and availability expectations are still based – at least implicitly – on the ideal type of male "normal biography" (cf. Geenen 1994; Jacobs/Winslow 2004; Knights/Richards 2003; Monday 2010). What is needed is therefore a job-centred one Lifestyle with a straightforward and complete professional biography. How from sandra Beaufaÿs (2003: 243) impressive described, becomes from scientists an undivided devotion to and complete identification cation with her Profession expected. As legitimate indicators for this, that persons this (apparently) also *live* , among other things such symbolically serve understanding practices such as full-time availability, working hours on end or the Coping longer and more insecure career paths (with one comparatively low income). attendance and time flexibility as well as monetary waivers are still considered stronger evidence of intrinsicsic Motivation, Determination and effort as one height Quality of work or high productivity despite limited (available) Time.

The fulfillment or. satisfiability this common and long-term "temporal performance indicators" directly affects the private life situation and way of life from scientists.

The scientific professional culture required the entire People and puts therewith the discharge "through a tacit background work" (for household and possibly children of care) as well as the unrestricted spatial and temporal flexibility acts ahead of another person – mostly the woman (cf. Beck-Gernsheim 1983; Moen/Roehling 2005). This creates the necessary time and spatial free spaces for the Partner, whose scientific Career Priority is to be physically fit for the job and job requirements and mental everywhere be available to can.

This professional-private "Balance" the division of labour is for the a for women who want to pursue a scientific career, as a rule not given and becomes for the others also for Men so partially throughquestioned the increase in academically educated female partners. beginning of In the 1970s, only one in seven graduates (aged 30 to 50) had Man in West Germany one academic educated partner (15%); in the In 2004 it was already one in three (in all of Germany; cf. Rusconi/ Solga 2007). Women with a college degree, on the other hand, had at that time like today, around half of them also have an academically educated partner. With the educational expansion between 1971 and 2004, the proportion of Academic partnerships from only 1% of all (West German) couples to 9% (All German) increased (Rusconi/Solga 2007: 312).

In addition, there is another interesting and relevant development tion on the pair context of academics. In 1971 every third woman lived with them an academic degree without a partner that men were with it only 11% (ie about every ninth). That proportion of singles stayed with the (30- to 50-year-old) women relatively constant over time, among men however, it rose to 27%. That is, even for academically educated people men today, almost every third is not through living with a Partner "tied" or "supported". This development may be aware that highly qualified men face increasing difficulties have, one "traditional" Woman to find, and or a increased interest

"Linked Lives" in Science

begin to establish themselves professionally before finding a partner shaft with one common Household and possibly with children enter.

German academic couples are often - and more often than couples with other their educational constellations – dual earner couples. The reason for this is the since the 1990s there has been a sharp increase in the labor force formed Women (see. Anger/Konegen-Grenier 2008). This regards also academy mike couples with children. In them waive Women today clearly less common to gainful employment than before. While in 1971 every second Aka- couple with at least one school-age or underage child only the man was employed, in 1997 this only applied to everyone third couple and in 2004 every fifth couple (Rusconi/Solga 2007: 319; 2004).

However, this does not mean that the two partners Double *earner* couples each have a career and thus *double realize* . Even in 2004, every fifth person (30 to 50 year olds) worked academically educated woman in a job that does not require a university degree (Rusconi/Solga 2007: 318). And so it can be stated that the Realization of dual careers in academic partnerships mostly restrictions the professional Development the Women fails.

In the Science, there are similar differences between men and women regarding support from an unpaid "back- basic work" or with regard to life in an academic partnership. While scientists on to the Away to the professorship more often as were men without a partner or mostly with an academically married man and in a dual-earner, if not dual-career arrangement gestures lived had her male Colleagues more often

Women without academic degree as well as A- or "only" dual earner arrangements. This is what a study on professors at German universities in Mitte shows the2000s that about 90% of the professors in a steady partnership lived but "only" 66% of their female colleagues (Room/Krimmer/Stallmann 2007: 148). Furthermore, although dual- *earner* arrangements for professors sorin How professors the majority life form represent, but while almost all partners of the professors were continuously employed, was after all almost a fifth of the partners of the professors (at least temporarily) not employed. After all, about a third of the partners were female professors also university teacher (at the professors were this only 5% of partners), while almost a quarter (23%) of their partners male colleagues have been teachers (Krimmer/Zimmer 2003: 29). This means that male and female scientists have very different different challenges and resources for the realization of a academic Career. So heard e.g. B. the teaching profession to those professions, which are in demand everywhere (cf. Cooke 2003); this makes the job search easier at one new Location, if the Pair because of *his* science career have to move. A survey of German universities from 2000 shows moreover, that university administrations saw themselves in a position, in particular, to support the job search of partners of newly appointed professors, if this teacher were (cf. Rusconi/Solga 2002; Solga/Rusconi 2004).

For women, a career in science is more often associated with restrictions when starting a family. Compared to university solvents in the general were scientists at German Universities much more often - also permanently - childless. during three quarter of all (over 43 years old) academically educated women had children, it was only half of the female scientists (Metz-Göckel/Selent/ Schuermann 2010: 20). [1] In addition, female scientists had fewer (and fewer) children than their male counterparts reclassify Difference that increases with age or career level. [2] im In 2006, two thirds of the professors were female, but only one third of the professors childless (see. Metz-Göckel/Selent/Schuermann 2010). [3] At the scientific central building (in the promotional or postdoc phase). the childlessness of women even higher (75%) - nevertheless in view of the lower age, some children were probably born here. Also here more men than women already have children, even if the difference between men and women in this career phase is less than at the professors. nevertheless have also Men in this Status passages often no children (yet) (71%). This high childlessness ability among men and above all among women at German universities the authors of the study on the special requirements and employ-conditions in the (German) science system return, the through long qualification paths and predominantly fixed-term employment contracts half the professorship marked are. Also ask she since End the 1990s a deterioration - an "increasing precarization" - the general conditions for scientific careers and with it increase

---

[1] The figures refer to Baden-Württemberg, Berlin, Brandenburg, Lower Saxony, North Rhine-Westphalia, Rhineland-Palatinate, Saxony and Thuringia, which together make up around 60% of the scientific staff of German universities (Metz-Göckel/Selent/ Schuermann 2010:18).

[2] In the case of the 21 to 29-year-old scientists, this gender difference was only one percentage point, compared to seven percentage points among 43 to 53-year-olds (Metz- Goeckel/Selent/Schuermann 2010: 20).

3   In the study by Zimmer, Krimmer and Stallmann (2007: 147f.) "only" one fifth of the professors, but half of the female professors are childless. In the latter there was a notable East-West difference: While almost all (albeit the very few) pro- female professors who had completed their doctorates in the GDR had children (94%), this applied to less than half of their West German colleagues (43%). See the explanations for this Authors in a different career logic for university careers in the GDR, which dem The principle of the "tenure track" followed, in a well-developed child care offer as well as in a lower attractiveness of science as a profession (Zimmer/Krimmer/ stableman 2007: 151f.).

"Linked Lives" in Science

end vulnerabilities, the one beginning a family confine   (can),   immovably   (Metz-Göckel/Selent/Schürmann 2010: 14). This assertion is subsequently reinforced that there is no proof that the longing to have kids is expanding qualified ladies varies from that of different ladies; in actuality, most of them, as well, actually need a bis two youngsters (see Part 3 in this book and Esping-Andersen 2009: 28).

Notwithstanding the functioning time designs and the monetary vulnerabilities in of science are likewise the orientation courses of action of associations ten from researchers no less huge variable for this, if and When Kids conceived become. Kids are for male researcher no issue "for however long they are on a customary orientation proportion in their confidential division of work" (Metz-Göckel/Selent/Schür-mann 2010: 10) - and undeniably more frequently than ladies they can return to fen. For instance, Zimmer, Krimmer and Stallmann (2007: 154) show that male teachers just in individual cases have the primary obligation regarding the consideration of their pre-younger students (2%) and just a minority on outside (private or public) mentoring

offers turned to has (7%)At two thirds became the Children
– "traditional" – mainly cared for by the partner. at the professor unsurprisingly, the picture was very different. They used too 40% private or public care offers; almost a fifth cared for their children mostly themselves, and at least another fifth the responsibility for child care was shared with the partner. The latter is a first indicator that academically educated men ners are increasingly being asked to take care of their children or want to be taken, so that they too have increased difficulties (become), the all-encompassing claim of male standardized scientific more To be able to (or to want).

1.3 *"Linked Lives" – Analytical Framework and questions of the book*

In summary, these historical and empirical developments fact that every tenth couple in Germany is an academic couple is - a trend that continues with the higher education of both men and women will increase (cf. Blossfeld/Timm 2003; Skopek/Schulz/Blossfeld 2009). It can also be observed that in many of these partnerships the women are more frequently employed and single-earner arrangements are on the wane, although she also still always not marginal are. Finally is to cons state that despite considerable investments in training by both partners , *pelcareerarrangements* no are a matter of course.

In view of these research findings and developments, the central The central thesis of this book is that the underrepresentation of women in leadership positions in science is also caused by the fact that Women the way to a professorship in connection with the professional career of their partner, i.e. as a *double career* , must succeed (since men on the one hand will probably not give up their careers and on the other hand a role barter and thus discrimination against men is not desirable result in terms of equality). Mindful of the fact that the vast majority of women and men in a partner community, renouncing a partnership for a career, if this at all is beneficial, no desired goal be.

However, dual careers are subject to specific challenges: on the one hand the temporal-spatial coordination of two - in the scientific shaft mostly longer term more insecure – careers and on the other hand the claims to be fulfilled at the same time with regard to partner and, if applicable, parent shaft. These reciprocal professional and private challenges can the

professional development opportunities partners mostly the Woman
– limit or prevent them altogether. Hence the career opportunities from (partnership bound) Women in mostly to sciencethe chances of realization Dual careers bound.

In contrast to other studies, which either only look at professional development of women (with and without children) compared to men or the Labour market- and organizational structures more professional careers we therefore systematically include the *couple level* in our with a. For this it is not enough to just identify the individual characteristics times of the two partners to be taken into account. Rather, the intertwining the professional development of both partners and the family division of work development to pay special attention to its dynamics (cf. Moen 2003). These interweaving and coordination arrangements are the result and at the same time central influencing factors for how couples deal with the social, cultural and institutional framework in their professional and handle family decisions. Even if external conditions are disadvantageous for women – with or without a partnership – so are they are by no means deterministic. For women in partnerships this means that their career opportunities are limited by internal couple arrangements and gender terrole attributions in of their Effect amplified or be reduced can. What intra-pair arrangements are there in terms of interweaving two professional careers and partnership with scientists in different career stages and what influence they have in the short and long term on the career opportunities of women in science is subject of the book.

"Linked Lives" in Science

When examining this thesis or the conditions for its realization of double careers of academically educated couples we assume one three-level model, in which career factors are based on the individual, external and couple-internal level, the professional development possibilities the both partner influence (see. Rusconi/Solga 2008; 2010). Career constellations and marriage arrangements of couples are through this reciprocal interaction the three levels however by no means stable (see Chapter 2 in this book). They are subject to those dynamics. These result from changing external requirements (due to changes in the labor market and organizational of careers inside and outside of science), through professional Transitions of one or both partners, through the birth of children as well ultimately by the termination and the new beginning of partnerships.

On the *individual level* influence processes the professional segregation the career opportunities of women and men - also completely independent of their involvement in a partnership (cf. also Krimmer/Zimmer 2003). As briefly outlined in Section 1.1, young ge women and men in their subjects. As is often the case in literature is occupied, combine with this horizontal segregation of the academic unequal career opportunities in the labor market (vertical segregation processes) in terms of pay, career patterns and opportunities for advancement (cf. e.g. Allmendinger/Podsiadlowski 2001; Anger/Konegen-Grenier 2008; England 2005). Access for women to managerial positions is about also - regardless of the field of study - through discriminatory practices ken by employers, e.g. B. by processes of statistical Discrimination, through which generalized in women from a low- higher productivity is assumed (cf. England 2005; Konrad/Cannings 1997; Reskin/Padavic 1994).

The Consequence are lesser opportunities for Women in recruitment for or promotion to leadership positions. These horizontal and vertical segregation processes are two further segregation processes intensified: informal and contractual differences in the employment of men and women. Show like this Studies that professional networks are segregated by gender and high qualified Women fewer in the "High trust" relationships professional networks included are (see. Allmendinger etc al. 1999; At the-sen/Oppen/Simon 1999; Wimbauer 1999). Women are not only lacking in formations above the career requirements and -criteria the mostly male selection committees for filling scientific economic positions; not only do they have fewer chances of that a "repute" that knows them in recruitment procedures gives them a perception mung of their Services and reputation gains provided. She have at the same time less opportunity to generate trust, which however one essential Pre-condition for cooperations or a professional one (loading) promotion is. In addition, the professional development opportunities Women are affected by often poorer contractual working conditions. They more often do their PhDs on scholarships; they rarely have a full-time job le (even if you wish); their employment contracts are more frequent and with shorter terms than men (cf. Metz-Göckel/Selent/ Schuermann 2010; Zimmer/Krimmer/Stallmann 2007). Also this restricts their professional integration and professional development opportunities (cf. e.g. Gash/Mcginnity 2007; Webber/Williams 2008).

These professional segregation processes lead – initially independently of whether women live in a partnership or not - too unequal Labour market- and career opportunities from Women and men. nevertheless they need for the internal couple relationships and interweaving arrangements by no means remain unaffected by two jobs. Because these different career prospects and positions on the labor market ten for (heterosexual) couple relationships that career opportunities in the Couple are unequally distributed and decisions in the couple for or against the affect the careers of one or the other.

On the *external couple level,* the professional opportunities of women and men influenced by being in a partnership live, move around on labor markets as a partner (and possibly parents). The Freedom of design and action for men and women in partner partnerships in which both partners (want to) pursue a career due to the temporal and spatial, often conflicting professional requirements struggles of the two partners as well as family requirements (cf. Rapoport/Rapoport 1969; sunrt 2005).

Job-related spatial mobility provides for academically educated Couples represent a central challenge (cf. Hess/Rusconi/Solga 2011a; Sonnet 2005). Academics move more often than average and life more often in multilocal life forms (everyday and weekend commuting and living-apart-together arrangements) because of spatial mobility an essential element of the professional development of persons with a an academic degree (cf. Becker et al. 2011; Büchel/Frick/Witte 2002; cutter et al. 2008). Result itself mobility requirements on- because of two careers, these are often in conflict with the stabilization family needs. It is then mostly the woman who looks at her Career forgone – especially when there are children (see below). And so it shows that women in partnerships and especially especially in those with children who are either less mobile than single people or move along with their partner more often (cf. Becker et al. 2011; Schneider et al. 2008).

A strategy used by couples when dealing with mobility is therefore, above all to look for jobs in regions where the two partners have good labor market tion promise (see. Costa/Kahn 2000; Moen/Wethington 1992). About it

"Linked Lives" in Science

In addition, employers (higher education le), such as job sharing, double hiring or support with the job search outside of the University, out of this Ground increasingly relevant
– especially at "isolated" university locations. Even if a employment at the same place can be advantageous for the partnership and family may, this does not necessarily have to be the case for career prospects of the two partners to be the case. Possibly the professional opportunities cen one or both partners better elsewhere, so the compromise at a place to life and to work, to professional restrictions for lead one or both partners and thus the realization of a long-term dual career can jeopardize (cf. Rusconi 2002).

The childcare offers also play a role on the couple-external level an important role. It depends very much on whether and in which Scope Couples with children can externalize care requirements (see intra-pair level below). In Germany in particular, the tongues for this very insufficient, there day schools in the Primary schoolare still not the norm, all-day kindergartens (until 5 p.m.) in many still represent an exception locally and for the statutory expansion of the crèche offer only a target of approx. 35% of the one to three-year-olds is provided. There is therefore a lack of public childcare required in general (cf. Plantenga et al. 2008) and especially at chen who with full-time and flexible working hours from two demanding professional activities compatible are. In addition is applicable normative always still the childcare as a responsibility of the mothers, such as the clear imbalance of the planned partner months, which called fathers months, since it is considered sufficient that the second parent only takes parental leave for two months (cf. Henninger/Wimbauer/Dombrowski 2008 as well as also Esping-Andersen 2009; Morgan/Zippel 2003).

With these general conditions become the Couples - above all the Women – career breaks or working time reductions to the compatibility from Profession and Family suggested. A such Compatible- However, the model of knowledge contradicts the logic of the career path in science society and the private sector that expect continuous employment biographies ten and frequently also age norms for the sequence from career steps as well as the Access to positions include. [4] But the Choice between Career breaks or working time reduction seems to be a choice between equivalent to cholera and plague. A career break strengthens e.g. B. the assumption of motivation deficits and strengthened when it affects women, gender stereotypes; it increases the risk of exclusion ses out of professional networks or the reproach "obsolete knowledge"

---

[4] to Part acts it itself included around by law fixed norms, How e.g. B. the age limit at the tenure.
(see above: individual level). A significant reduction in working time (e.g. to 50%) might not be a good alternative for a number of reasons. visible the career opportunities represent. On the one hand contradicts part time the full-time ideal of scientific careers and can also be used as a motivation deficit are interpreted. Even the often encountered contractual chen part-time positions while the promotion regarding only the Pay, but not the expected working time. part-time professorships family reasons are also scarce. Existing part-time professorships are mostly due to (remunerative) part-time jobs ten, so that the "willingness to work" of the owners is not called into

question becomes. For the others becomes part time in the qualification phase fined, then for the crediting of the years according to the twelve-year rule schen universities is the contractual working time (i.e. how many hours being worked) irrelevant. At the same time, however, the provision becomes the same Qualification achievements in the same period - despite possibly different ones working hours – expected.

Set the influencing factors of the individual and the couple-external level the framework conditions in which women and men in academic couple their – common or individual – familial and professional ones Make decisions. The named unequal treatment of women and men on labor markets, the frequently contradictory temporal spatial requirements of scientific careers as well as the institutional nell and organizational Conditions from Work or. Science and family do place restrictions on the scope for creativity pairs, but in no way do they necessarily mean that academic mixedly educated women in these couples forgo their professional careers ten must. How the respectively existing freedom of design used becomes,

ie how couples deal with these demands and conflicts is also depending on the gender roles of the two partners,

the respective interpretation of the external conditions by the two partners as well as the associated and practiced interdependence and coordination arrangements of the couple.

In this respect, with the *internal couple level, there are* also intra-partnerships Negotiation processes and coordination strategies related to work – Career – Family in The invoice to place. In them become the on the both conditions created on other levels and thereby processed the potency of those factors in enabling or loading or. prevention from dual careers co-determined.

Out of the present- the Research permit itself in this regard essentially three intertwining ment of professional careers in partnerships that the couple-internal interpretations and power relations of the external career Opportunities reflect: a) hierarchical, b) individualistic and c) egalitarianmodes of interweaving.

"Linked Lives" in Science

With *hierarchical interdependencies,* a partner becomes – mostly the man - attributed the primary professional role, and the other partner - mostly the woman – supports his career by being responsible for theprivate matters. If both partners are employed, there is a definition tion of a "leading" and a "following" occupation, the work requirements in terms of working hours and spatial mobility/stability Requirements the leading Career subordinate become. The is called, professional decisions of subordinate professional activities are made to the viewing angle the Career of others partners as well as of living together on the same place met (cf. e.g. Becker/Moen 1999).

With *individualistic ways of intertwining,* both partners pursue because independently their professional careers. The partnership, ie the time together and possibly living in one place, here comes a secondary role too. Long-distance or commuting relationships represent a possible one here (although not necessarily desired) coordination strategy towards look at the career opportunities for both partners. With the birth of Individualistic coordination arrangements not only appear to falter because of this local distance. Pair-external as -internal come with parenthood, gender-specific role expectations back to the Surface. It is then up to the two partners to decide whether they meet expectations or whether they are looking for external or shared childcare looking for opportunities. The research here shows that temporary thought Concessions (mostly on the part of women) in this circumstance are gigantic convey the gamble of long haul negative vocation results. does it come in this manner prompting a "renewal" of customary orientation job attributions practices likewise in the expert circle, then, at that point, in the drawn out it turns into a progressive examples of intra-familial division of work among work and family gone

(cf. Demand/Ernst 2002; Schulz/Blossfeld 2006). ladies who a need to keep an individualistic model of reliance conceivably to kids or delay the longing to have youngsters until she her vocation goals Satisfies or not more imperiled see (kindly allude Segment 1.2 and Sections 3 and 4 in this A book).

Obviously more uncommon as individualistic methods of joining gives it regardless of tary coordination plans in organizations. Considering the circumstances, they harbor the peril that the two accomplices for living respectively (in the feeling of shared general setting) will make slices and splits the difference as to their own vocations make (see. Bathmann/Müller/Cornelissen 2011; Becker/Moen 1999; Behnke/Meuser 2005). For the drawn out acknowledgment of a comparability of Vocation, organization and conceivable life as a parent would hence must be confined if essential. of the vocations of the two accomplices are acknowledged or might corresponding likely for the family at some point be   depleted.

Questions and structure of the book

The interest in higher education and science policy in dual careers is increased significantly - and a lot is being done to achieve this. So had for example one growing number German universities *dual careers Offices* set up (cf. e.g. Gramespacher/Funk/Rothhäusler 2010). In addition, lie research findings to dual career couples out of the numerous (also German) studies that have been created in the last ten years. Thus, for one or the other at this point, perhaps the Ask the question: Why this book? Don't we already know everything? The simple The answer is: we need this book because we don't know everything by a long shot. There are numerous research gaps, which we will not cover in this book can close. We will therefore focus on some, albeit very (must) limit open questions. [5]

Unknown are in view of the above-mentioned tension ratio- ses of challenges and different influencing factors in relation on scientific careers in (Academic) partnerships (a) the *Dynamics of interdependence arrangements* with regard to employment (single vs. dual earners) in male and female scientists and (b) what role therein career changes or the birth of children play. The following open questions are connected with this: Are double earning arrangements easier in earlier phases of the professional biography accomplish than in later ones, since on the one hand the temporal-spatial challenges requirements in the career history gain weight and on the other hand the Familys- founding often only takes place after professional establishment? how important ting is what interweaving pattern the two partners before the first Have practiced for how the arrangement after the birth of the child child looks? And finally: Permit itself differences in intertwining development patterns and their dynamics between younger and older birth vintages, and if so, do they lead to greater equality between male and female scientists? this one central questions Chapter 2 of this book is dedicated to this.

For the connection between child and career everything seems to be the same to be said or researched. But the following are still unanswered Questions: What influence do *the care strategies pursued in the couple have? gi and practiced care arrangements for her Children* on the knowledge-academic careers of women? What negotiation processes between the both partners lay the respectively practiced care patterns actually perish? And are the career opportunities – as many assume – really better if the birth of the first child is postponed is, or are the couple's internal care arrangements more related with (external) care services through Third crucial? This

---

5   for further aspects please refer Hess/Rusconi (2010); Hess/Rusconi/Solga (2011a, b).

"Linked Lives" in science

Questions are answered in Chapter 3. Special attention will thereby – with a comparison on the one hand of female scientists with and without children and on the other hand by mothers with and without a career – the overarching Ask given, in which case Children not to one
"career break", but to a continuation of the scientific careerre of women (can) lead.

In the Research becomes moreover always still of that went out, that women are less career-oriented or their professional success in it see that work and family can be easily reconciled. Unasked remains but why women may have a different *definition of career and success* as men. What role does the individual and made in pairs play Processing of external framework conditions (see individual level and match outside level above) for the profession direction of researchers no? This is the focal inquiry that the creators seek after in Part 4. In doing as such, they look at which historical directions for Separations of female researchers in the field of pressure of science and Family activity directing were. Which vocation disservices from Ladies in science are expected by ladies and their accomplices, and how would you approach arranging your profession and life as a team to? To address these inquiries, this section just effective female researchers, for example the individuals who, at the hour of the Between sees have a vocation (see Segment 1.5), contrasted with one another similitudes, yet additionally the inner change of "effective" profession directions in light of two or three groups of stars and encounters quality with to have the option to show outside structure conditions.

At last, the inquiry emerges: How significant are the long haul commonsense ticated examples of association of prior stages - which are managed in Section 2 become - for the later vocation and double profession chances of information laborers? Does progress in science truly require a careful normal expert history à la typical male memoir? Will sub refractions for the most part fined? Become versatility or multilocal private game plans compensated? Addressing these inquiries, Part 5 goes into The justification for the central issue: Is the "masculinization" of female life Is there at present the main street to progress for ladies, or is there past of the vocation legend (cf. Moen 2010; Moen/Roehling 2005) individual Two or three techniques that additionally offer open doors for ladies' vocations in science shaft and double professions in open pair?

Reply on this Questions should eventually furthermore contribute figure out What useful Circumstances or "Achievement Conditions" from science-normal professions of ladies - and the related twofold vocations - are and to what extent factors that we often consider to be particularly important perhaps are not that important.

1.4 Linked Lives by who? - Data basis ofbook

The book is based on a unique database consisting of quantitative ve and qualitative interviews that were collected as part of the project the. For answering our research questions and closing the research gaps mentioned above, it is necessary, on the one hand, to having scientists living in a couple context, and on the other hand, to have information about both partners, which the partners respectively self given become. Straight information for the Life course of the partners before the partnership as well as subjective assessments tongues regarding division of labour or career ambitions can not out of
be given "third-hand". Such a data set previously existed in the Federal Republic not.

There are now a number of qualitative studies on double fur careers or. to the Intertwining of professional careers in partnerships (cf. e.g. Behnke/Meuser 2005; Dettmer/Hoff 2005; Hirseland/Herma/ Schneider 2005; Wimbauer 2010). However, their significance is due to the mostly very small number of cases and the very specific nature of each case samples limited. The existing population-representative data sentences are also not sufficient for examining dual career mate. Although the microcensus offers a very large number of cases (also at Aka- demic couples), it gives however barely information to the identification from Dual careers or the place of work of both partners. through its transverse cut design, acquisition constellations in partnerships are also only as punctual phenomenon detectable. Intra-partnership negotiation pro- processes and decision-making situations cannot be reconstructed. For the Investigation from academic partnerships is the case count in theexisting representative longitudinal studies, i.e. in the socio-economic schen Panel (SOEP) of the

German Institute for Economic Research or in the German Life Course Studies of the Max Planck Institute for Educationresearch, too little. In addition, they would usually do so if the number of cases was higher not help, because e.g. B. Housing arrangements of the two partners in are not collected in connection with the two professional biographies or became. However, the latter in particular can be considered a central component of internal partnership interweaving arrangements not disregarded be allowed (see Chapter 5 in this book). Furthermore, the average conducting independent qualitative interviews with scientists their partners - linked back to a larger number of cases - not possible been.

"Linked Lives" in science

sample design and content the quantitative survey

But collecting your own data is easier said than done. Because there is no register for scientists - and certainly not not one, in to the the partnership status registered were –, on whoseBased on that, a sampling would have been possible. In the project we have therefore chosen the following path: the survey institute Infas Bonn has in the summer semester 2008 one research the employee directorieson the websites of 18 selected universities (in big cities and medium-sized cities with large universities). for one large number of social, technical and natural science departments (without medicine) a list of persons and a (as far as possible first) classification according to career levels. On this basis followed one random draw within the after Gender, career level, discipline and regional context defined cells (see table 1.1).

In the 2008/09 winter semester, a standardized telephone Life Course Interview (CATI) from infa carried out in Bonn. Only scientific employees were questioned of universities that have been in a permanent partnership for at least two years shaft lived and whose Partners (for the time of interview) also a had college degrees.

In the telephone interviews, detailed information on all learners was schooling and college degrees and for the period starting from the principal College degree gathered up to the hour of the meeting and month to month Exact data on movements of every sort of the expert life story (incl. interferences because of bringing up youngsters, joblessness or different exercises ten) and all associations and kids (remembering data for youngsters care until for the 6th Age). What's more for each episode this expert account the transcendent private, profitable pay and gets some information about the couple's work-sharing game plan; further subtleties focal system conditions and choice groups of stars.

Numerous this data can not or not solid (without "legitimization" processes) review, ie in the knowing the past, raised become. Hence, researchers were reviewed at four profession levels, around so as "close" as conceivable to the separate choice circumstances to be:

1. not graduated representatives (PhD understudies);

2. doctorate, whose advancement most extreme three Years lingered behind

3. doctorate, whose advancement more as three Years falled behind and Junior-teachers;

4. Professors (C3/C4 and W2/W3).

Since the data on the association isn't and on the profession level not generally current or obviously on sites open are, became over a short Starting screening guarantees that the individual meets the examining measures (logical representative of these colleges, for no less than two years in an organization with somebody who is likewise scholastically taught accomplice alive and characterization in one of the four vocation levels). furthermore, was able to give a contact telephone number to her partner teln (since the partner interview was also important for the study, see above). If this was the case, a (full) interview was conducted. After the interview was completed, the partner for the permanent standardized partner interview and the target persons for a qualitative tives Interview selected (see below).

Table 1.1: Realized interviews with scientists and their Partners by career level, gender and discipline (absolute number)

M = Men, f = Women
Source: record "Together Career make"; own calculations

For each of the four career levels were for men and women and the three Discipline groups each 30 or for professors 35 standard ted interviews aimed at (in total 750 interviews). In addition should 500 standardized interviews are conducted with their partners. realised became ultimately 767 interviews with scientists and 552 with their partners. However, not all groups could target number of cases can be reached (see Table 1.1). This applies in particular especially the group of women professors in technical sciences (at those the universe already extreme small is) as well as the group the

"Linked Lives" in Science

Scientists whose doctorate was no more than three years ago. last tere could largely with interviews of the doctorate, their doctorate more than three years ago, to be compensated.

The place of work and the employment or non-employment of the Partners the questioned scientists had to not in the be in college or in academia. This means that very different che constellations are compared: both partners in science (scientifically homogeneous couples); one partner in and one outside of science senschaft employed (occupational heterogeneous couples); a partner in science society and the other partner not employed (single-earner couples in the Science). Are not taken into account in our analyzes - if they itself on the Get the time of the interview – so "only" dual earner and single-earner couples outside of academia, as well as couples in which both partner not employed are. Alles this constellations can nevertheless for the period *before* the interview also in the case of the ten appear in pairs and with it taken into account become.

The same applies to the selection criterion "Living in a partnership". At the time of the interview, the scientists we interviewed had a partnership for at least two years. However, that does not conclude out of, that she in the times before intermittently none partner had. In the Data-The only data not included are those who at the time of the interview either temporarily had no partner or (until the time of the interview) never in lived in a partnership. It is difficult to say how large this proportion is estimate, because there is no reliable database to calculate this (see above). Nonetheless, given the proliferation of partnerships It can also be assumed for university graduates that with this reference sample a more substantial Portion the at colleges working Knowledge- schaftler and the majority the there make scientists recorded become (see section 1.2).

The standardized Life Course Interviews became for the Chapter of book in more diverse Way descriptive and multivariate evaluated. Included permit itself two important evaluation strategies differentiate:

(a) *historical* evaluations for the individual career history the Scientists or on the interweaving arrangements in the couple (e.g. realized as distribution graphics of the respective individual or in pairs Career status over a certain period of time and evaluations using sequence and regression analyses) and (b) *event-related* evaluations (e.g. until a doctorate or one of the next career steps in the Postdoc phase – see Section 1.5

- also, when the introduction of youngsters).

In the elucidating assessments - on the off chance that they are not subject-explicit fish are - was considered by a comparing weighting that different case numbers for the three discipline bunches present. Bezo gen z. B. on the general example are among the ladies from the inherent sciences logical subjects with 139 meetings a bigger number of meetings than from the sociologies (128) and specialized sciences (96) chern. Among men, there is a slight lion's share of sociologies schaftler (140) contrasted with the specialized and regular researchers (134 and 130). Comparable contrasts additionally exist when individual vocation gatherings or just those cases are assessed in which meetings of the part-ners are accessible. Given different profession rationales in these three subject gatherings (cf. Hess/Rusconi/Solga 2011a), an unweighted te utilization of the information in unmistakable examines lead to the Rationales of the disciplines that are addressed with higher case numbers through would hit and in this way the generalizability would be restricted. In the engaging examines go into the singular instances of the three disciplines bunches hence with an alternate weight, which guarantees that no gathering is overweight or that each of the three gatherings contribute similarly to the outcome. In the multivariate examinations, this inconsistent number of cases by assessing comparing coefficients proper considered.

Design and content the qualitative survey

The second part of the project was a qualitative survey with a Selection carried out by scientists and their partners. Against- The status of these qualitative interviews were the subjective planning behavior, the inner-partner action strategies and evaluation dimensions, the negotiation processes in the couple as well as the anticipations, interpretations and Processing of the institutional environmental factors of scientific careers between partnership and family. At the end of the *standard* For this reason, all interview partners became *dis- tributed life course interviews* around her approval to one further survey asked. The granted 96% of the scientists and 97% of the part- very high. Ultimately, the real willingness to participate in a qualitative interview somewhat lower. Of the 47 knowledge workers could 33 for a interview won become. About it In addition, as planned, twelve interviews were conducted with partners from this science carried out.

All scientists who were willing to participate in the panel were introduced sampling procedures into the selection for the qualitative interviews included. The groups defined therein contrast with regard to theoretical Retically established criteria, with a variation of these categories maximum heterogeneity of the feature combinations is represented in the sample ("model of deliberate sampling of heterogeneity" after Campbell/Cook 1979). After to the from Glaser/Strauss (1967) formulated saturation principle

"Linked Lives" in Science

for qualitative interviews suffice ten to twelve theme-centric interviews with experts in the subject area to be explored, as further inter- views do not provide any additional information relevant to the topic. This Comparison group construction allows later contrasting case studies same certain subgroups (cf. Kluge/Kelle 2001).

headquarters selection criteria were the Couple career constellation for the Time of interview and discipline affiliation. at the couple career constellation (for the interview time the standardized marriage exercise) we have distinguished the following groups: (a) female scientists, at those both partner one Career have (ie dual career couples, n=15), (b) women scientists, where only the man (n=9) or (c) only the woman had a career (n=9). Of the 33 women interviewed en were eleven female professors, 24 of the women had children and nine had (yet) none. In addition, the subject and occupational field constella-tion of the couples at the time of the standardized interview. 14 women with a scientifically homogeneous partner and 19 Women interviewed with a professionally homogeneous partner. most knowledge at the time of the interview were in the group of pro-promoted, whose doctorate was more than three years ago. Over and beyond "Freshly" doctorates (career level 2) and female professors also became questioned.

The interviewed partners of twelve of these scientists were selected according to the following criteria: Age between 30 and 49 years (or born between 1960 and 1979), from dual career and single career couples as well as couples with a typical and egalitarian division of labor in the home just. In addition, all three discipline groups and partners are involved professional activities inside and outside of science represent The survey of the qualitative interviews followed the strategy created in the SFB 186 ckelten technique for issue focused interviews (cf. Witzel 2000). On based on an aide with an inventory of points that guarantees that all fascinating subjects are tended to and, if vital, followed up are asked, this sort of interview permits the focus on pre-characterized ones Branches of knowledge and impacting factors. By connecting open story prompts with dialogic testing arrangements, the Connection on specific Vocation and organization stages take, offers this Interview structure sufficient room for self-promotion of the interviewees. About the memory work and recreation of the genuine sequencing of the profession and relationship gradually eases in the meeting has been dispensed with the information of the quantitative study for every interviewee individual history outline made. The meetings zeroed in on those there recorded groupings, the intrigued (institutional) apparent

"defining moments" and other emotionally critical "defining moments". This Procedures the archive based summarization permits one generally excellent Association from quantitative Life History Information and subjective designs of importance.

headquarters characteristics the questioned scientists

At the time of the interview, the standardized questioned scientists were point ever after career level (in the median) between meager 29 and 54 years old (Tabel 1.2). At the professors gave it clear age schiede: On average, female professors were six years younger than male professors (this indicates an even greater underrepresentation of women in earlier generations). At the first university degree were the male Scientists at all career levels on average 26 years old, run a year younger. In the median, the scientific students and professors in their early 30s, ie about five years after (first) university degree, doctorate. Here, too, there was hardly any gender differences. The situation is different with the habilitation. She was from the Professors - median - 14 years after graduation ben, by the female professors after 15.5 years.

.

The *median* gives information about the age, until in addition at 50% of samples the respective "Event" has occurred. In contrast to the arithmetic mean (average) is the median not prone to extreme cases. In addition, he allows for events that (still) not at everyone persons of samples happened have (e.g. B. birth of first child or habilitation), the entire sample for the calculations to take into account.

M = Men, f = Women

Source: record "Together Career make"; own calculations

"Linked Lives" in Science

As the duration of the partnerships at the time of the interview shows, it is acting are long-term couple relationships. The attachment to a partner was already widespread at the beginning of one's professional career. Almost three four part of all scientists were already alive when they received their first university degreein a partnership; in three quarters of them it lasts (did) until the inter- view time. The women scientists surveyed lived a little more often in a partnership than their male counterparts (78% vs. 71%) as well a little more often with the same partner during their - from the first University degree observed up to the time of the interview – professional career (79% of women vs. 74% of men). This high proportion of (longtime) partnerships is partially the sample construction owed. People who have never lived in a partnership or for longer Times without a partner were, had none or a statistically lower Chance of being included as a target person in the survey (see above). Nevertheless, this is not a shortcoming for the analyses, since it is precisely with the interweaving from professional biographies *in the partnership* a research deficitexists (see Section 1.3) and this the subject of the book is.

The scientists were approximately 23 Months

(median) younger as their partners, scientists, conversely, eleven months older than their partners- to. With half of the scientists, the partner was still studying when he had already completed their studies (vs. 31% of female scientists, the to time of their partner's university degree).

With regard to the children, there were only clear ones among the professors Differences: 85% of the professors were fathers (on average of two children dern), but "only" 61% of the female professors had (on average) a child. Three quarters of the scientists with a doctorate had (at least) one Child; among doctoral students, on the other hand, three quarters did not (yet) have any (biological) children. For the time of the birth of the first child there is same to you clear differences as well as between the as also within of career stages: 50% of women with doctorates had their first child by seven years after her first university degree and thus two years earlier than their male counterparts. In contrast, the pro- fessorinnen the birth of the first child on average twelve years after academic degree and thus four years later as at your colleagues instead.

These differences between the career stages are a further points out that women with children have a harder time in science. The reduction in the proportion of children, as well as the increase in age, when these children were born to the female professors compared to the Graduates are indicators that post-docs are female scientists have poorer chances of getting a professorship with (early) children men. This interpretation seems to be appropriate as the age difference differed between the female PhD students and female professors only average ten Years amounts to (please refer Table 1.2). Therewith were it very question lich, this differences as "Generational Differences" to interpret. The findings for the (older) female professors are therefore not only aimed at them restrict. Rather, they can also be used to derive a more frequent "Aus- rose" from the science of women with children in the (younger) pro- moved anticipate (see also chapter 3 in this A book).

meaningfulness the data

The Data, used for the analyzes in this book not representative of all academics at German universities. To put it positively, stand the results for following Groups of people:

- Individuals with a college degree who have at least a certain Time (at least at the time of the interview) at one of the 18 selected Universities (in Big and medium-sized cities) were busy;
- Scientists who have had at least a two-year partnership withone also academic had educated partners;
- scientists out of disciplines the Technology-, Nature- and Social Sciences (for reasons of anonymity we refrain from given qualitative interviews on the naming of the selected specializations in this three discipline groups).

This study group is responsible for answering the questions formulated above Questions of the book on *scientific careers in (heterosexual) partnerships* very suitable. 6 The consideration of the three disciplines nen – technology (strongly male-dominated), natural (male-dominated) and Social Sciences (mixed to male dominated) – also protects against disciplinary shortenings due to different career logics or gender proportional realities.

Some also go with this construction of the study population restrictions. Firstly, we are dealing with more of a positive choice of people with regard to staying in academia. All People who – for whatever reason – generally oppose the science have decided are not included in the sample (although "Returnees" are included who on occasion - before the overview - are not were in science). The exit from science can accordingly can't be inspected straightforwardly , however exclusively by contrasting the qualities male of the gatherings of doctoral understudies, postdocs and teachers occur (see the model above for youngsters). It ought to be recalled call, that researchers the never (yet) had an association or whose accomplice doesn't have a college degree, isn't essential for the populaces are (kindly allude above). Besides have in our example

6 interviews with researchers in same two or three connections remain in light of the to low case include in the examinations this book dismissed.

"Linked Lives" in Science

more scientists children than in other studies, since we only have those who live in a partnership and are therefore more likely to also likely to have children as singles. Finally we can third make no statements on the humanities and cultural studies as well as on small universities in which not all three disciplines are represented, and to smaller towns. Failure to take this into account is pragmatic in terms of research cal reasons, ie the cost limitation with regard to the number of cases, owes.

1.5 Dual Career - What is it?

In both older and more recent studies, *dual career couples are* seldom made explicit and uniformly defined and operationalized (cf. Hiller/Dyehouse 1987; Saraceno 2007). With it is the comparability more different for Research results about different study populations and the Only possible to a limited extent over time. This fact is however fewer one "Carelessness" the researchers owed rather largely the real problem of defining what actually is is a career (cf. Moen 2003; 2010), and along with that also what one dual career is. In this respect, we will not become a universally valid one definition give can, nevertheless would like we our definition disclose and justify.

First of all, let's take a look at the deficits of the existing definitions or operationalizations from dual careers sensible. First become (still) often dual *career* couples with dual *earner* couples equated (cf. e.g. Aldous 1982; Bernasco/De Graaf/Ultee 1998; Blossfeld/Drobnič 2001). This means that any participation in (paid) gainful employment – regardless of level, career level or other characteristics of the activity carried out – a "career".

Second, even in studies that make such a distinction, there are no uniform criteria for defining a *career* . Used very different structural characteristics of the employed ability, such as professional position (cf. e.g. Gross 1980; Lucchini/Sarace- no/Schizzerotto 2007), the level of education required to exercise a activity (cf. e.g. Rusconi/Solga 2007) or practicing a profession (cf. e.g. Bryson/Bryson 1980; Dettmer/Hoff 2005; Poloma/Pendelton/Gar- country 1981).

Third, subjective indicators often become real ones career derived. This is how some authors define career based on subjective career attitudes or ambitions - often summarized under to the Expression of "job commitment" (for one criticism please refer Hiller/Dye house 1987; Levy/Bühlmann/Widmer 2007) - and set this with the reality equalization of careers.

Fourth, some authors rightly point out that Careers should not be defined statically, but dynamically as one development, which, however, happens very rarely. Therefore, the card should definition of the consideration of the (previous) overall biography and its Include cumulativeness and direction of development (cf. Bielby/Bielby 1984; Hiller and Dyehouse 1987; Levy/Bühlmann/Widmer 2007).

This variety of definition criteria and their operationalization is also to the original career definition of Rapoport and Rapoport (1969). Define dual careers in the first post they careers (in contrast to employment) as "jobs which are high- ly salient personally, have a developmental sequence other require a high degree of commitment" (Rapoport/Rapoport 1969: 3). In the previous However, only individual dimensions are taken into account in the calculation, and only rarely is the multidimensional nature of careers formulated here implemented.

In addition, it is discussed whether dual careers apply to *couples* or relate *families* . The title of the first study by Rapoport and Rapoport (1969) on dual careers did not refer to the couple but to "The Dual career *families* ". Here examined she so couples, at those both (marriage) partner one Career *and* at least a child had. One newer study defines children as a *condition* of dual careers - with the justification ment that only through "the associated duties and the 'family arbeit'" the professional careers of both partners would be difficult to realize (Cle- ment/Clement 2001: 255). Out of this perspective have we it so to say with one double dual career to do: the realization two Professional careers and their connection with the birth and upbringing of children. This definition is however out of two Found problematic. First becomes with it the relationship and housework of couples without children a priori as "a academic subject" devalued; Secondly becomes on this Way normative set, that Children belong to a (perfect) couple relationship, because childless couples could by definition no dual career have. It gives so but not only numerous studies for different countries that show that the Birth of children, women's chances for gainful employment and Careers – and consequently the likelihood of dual careers – reduced (cf. e.g. Levy/Bühlmann/Widmer 2007; Levy/Ernst 2002; Luc-Chini/Saraceno/Schizzerotto 2007; Rusconi/Solga 2007; Schulz/Blossfeld 2006). There is just as much evidence that the interdependence of two professional biographies *without* children is neither a matter of course nor uncomplicated or. always successful is (see. e.g. B. Becker/Moen 1999; Bielby/Bielby 1992; Hertz 1986; Small 1996; Rusconi/Solga 2007). The often with careers related requirements in temporal and more spatial There-

"Linked Lives" in Science
Visibility is not just a major challenge for couples when they are children (please refer Sections 1.2 and 1.3 and the further chapter of this book).

definition of career and dual career in this A book

given this research and discussion situation differentiate we in this A book explicit between employment and Career. The nakedness Although gainful employment is a necessary requirement, it is not sufficient characteristic for the existence of a career. For this sub use divorce we use the following criteria.

As first must it itself around the exercise one *educationally adequate* activity, ie the activity performed must match the previously acquired match qualifications. In this respect, it is not the income, but the job content decisive.

Secondly is – How already from report and report (1969) executed

– the prospect of *professional (further) development* is important. careers in different professions, areas of activity and economic sectors consequences that is different logics and Requirements regarding career patterns and professional cultures; However, what they all have in common is that they include advancement opportunities. This also corresponds to the career definition tion of the dictionary of a (fast, successful) professional career, a professional advancement and the underlying French Word "carrière" (race track, career) (cf. Drosdowski 1989). accordingly Accordingly, careers must be defined *longitudinally in order to* ven and upward changes in *qualification , professional to be able to observe position* and *social advancement* . the existing be a career is therefore based on the realized professional Development or the prospect of it *according to* the life. or better defined by this institutional age (see below). So would e.g. B. a place in of the science on which doctorate can be obtained, five years after Completion of studies in line with your career, but not ten years later.

Children as well as "job commitment" and career ambitions become as definition criterion from us not taken into account. She can surely represent important influencing factors for the realization of careers - what however, would have to be tested empirically (Levy/Bühlmann/Widmer 2007: 264; see also chapters 3 and 4 in this book); however, they define themselves not, if one professionally, in the senses a career is successful or not.

These considerations result in the following operationalization of the Career concept in this book, which is also based on the data collected standardized interviews could be implemented. Are these criteria If the criteria are met by both partners, there are *dual careers* accordingly before. Figure 1.2 shows our key criteria for careers in science according to science to the institutional age and the career level.

Note: T_0 defines the time of the first study connection, T_6 stands for "six Years after graduating" etc.

With regard to the *acquisition of qualifications,* six years after the first university degree, the doctorate and 16 years later the habilitation tion are available (see lower part of Figure 1.2). A junior professorship was defined as adequate up to a maximum of 17 years after graduation ned. If you look at those who have (already) found a professorship have achieved (with the doctorate after five years on average and the Habilitation after twelve years, see Table 1.2), we give with these threshold values somewhat "more time" compared to the career logic coming under pressure (cf. also Zimmer/Krimmer/Stallmann 2007:103). (Yet) longer periods of time for achieving this career- steps represent a "deviation from the prevailing norm" and probably also go with disadvantages in terms of further professional Development or career.

Regarding the *educationally adequate professional position* (upper Part from Figure 1.2) are highly qualified jobs or scientific al employee positions with the appropriate salaries or allowances (at least BAT IIa, TVL or TVöD 13, A13 or C1) asbasis the definition

taken. PhD grants become until at most six Years after to the academic degree and habilitation scholarships until ten Years thereafter as career compliant considered. Ten Years

"Linked Lives" in Science

after to the scholarly degree would it be a good idea for one certain freedom or. obligation regarding execution has been accomplished. For this reason, the basis "The executives of undertakings with somewhere around one worker (incl. understudy laborers)". At last, a period cutoff of 18 years after graduation for moving to an extremely durable residency or chief position or comparative given; ie every one of the people who are still in science from that point onward, yet not on such Position were delegated "non-vocation" around then. In the here present Information changed the addressed teachers previously something before - 15 Years after her most memorable scholarly degree (middle)

-        on her most memorable residency or chief position (see. additionally room/blood red/ stableman 2007: 103).

Also, for proficient exercises beyond the Science Profession measures or dates by which the procurement from administrative roles ought to be characterized.

1.6 *Our Record: Obstacles to and Realization conditions of dual careers in academic partnerships*

In section 1.3 a number of open research questions were formulated, which are answered in the following chapters. concern of our accounting at this Job is it, based from important findings out of this Chapters summarize the central question of the book "What are Obstacles to and what are the conditions for the realization of scientific chen careers of women and the associated double careers in Academic partnerships?".

Our initial thesis was that dual careers in academic partner partnerships are fragile arrangements that can be changed at any time by parties outside the partnership and internal factors (see Section 1.3) can be questioned. Because who sets the "tone" in these partnerships - he, she or both - or what the rhythm of the career paths of the two partners looks like the mutual result of the institutions of the labor market or the scientific system, whose interpretations and processing in the partnership and the resulting intra-partnership practices interweaving arrangements. The latter also represent the "interconnected systems" the gendered status biographies the both partner in Education, Labor market and family and thus contribute to a (re)production or reduction the inequalities in the career opportunities from Women and men inside and outside of the partnership. However, how do these composite systems out of, and which Influence have she on the realizationof dual careers?

Chapter 2 shows that *dual earner* arrangements both in pro- motions as well as in the postdoc phase with 55% and 58% respectively weave way the from us examined academic partnerships are. Included consist striking differences between Women and men

— but not between the disciplines, so that the

different share in the respective professional Surroundings on it has no influence. A *first* difference is that already in the doctoral phase Sole earner constellation, in which only the man is employed, with the men significantly more frequently and to a considerable extent. find is (35% vs. 13% among women), while women 66% in a living in a dual earner constellation. This difference is evident in couples with and without children alike; it is therefore not due to the employment refraction from Women through Children caused. That this differences in the employment constellations of the pair of scientists scientists are relatively independent of the presence of children also remember that there is a high degree of stability in the modes of interweaving before and after birth of children there.

Secondly, female scientists live much more frequently in double wages nerarrangements than their male counterparts. That is, scientific women have to follow their professional career goals much more often than men match the job requirements of their partners. An important prerequisite The reason for this is certainly that you and your partners in the long term - in the doctoral tion *and* postdoc phase – a dual earner arrangement practice. This succeed one relative huge Portion. More as the half the couples, the in the doctoral phase in a scientifically homogeneous dual-income arrangement lived led this away (57%), and further 13% became Occupationally heterogeneous double earner couples, in which predominantly the man left science after completing his doctorate. A similar pattern shows up for the partnerships of women who are in the doctoral phase occupational heterogeneity arrangement practiced have.

Thirdly, the sole gainful employment of the man if children are are just as widespread among scientists at 40% as dual earner arrangements. However, female

scientists also live on the birth of children mostly (more than 50%) in a double income arrangement. The means that scientific careers for women must in clearly stronger Dimensions under the Conditions, not the Support
"one tacit background work" of partners to have (see. Beck Gernsheim 1983) and at the same time the challenges of two employment reconciling activities and childcare can be realized. Men however start not only more often as sole earner her Career, rather

"Linked Lives" in Science

42% remain so in the phase after the doctorate or beyond entire career. Only a third of them switched to a double pelverinnererarrangement. Nevertheless, it should be emphasized that men, if they because living in a partnership with a female scientist, even in stronger to a large extent with the challenges of realizing double income nerarrangements, such as the findings on the scientific show gutters

However, if the relatively high proportion of double-income couples, especially especially among female scientists, also to - for the scientific important careers of women – *dual careers* ? First is It should be noted that despite the significant investments in dual careers Studies and doctorate as well as dual employment are not automatically place. The findings in Chapter 5 show that twelve years after the Graduation only 53% the scientists and 40% the Knowledge- schaftler had a dual career as a couple. However, while the Most of the scientists (namely 86%) nevertheless have a career was able to accomplish (although 45% as the only one in the pair), could only 73% of female scientists (with 20% as the sole career in Pair). This one – in view of the high level of education and labor force participation of both Partner – but high proportion of male careers prioritized in pair (45% in the partnerships of scientists and 23% in the scientists) was to beginning the professional career – i.e. H. in the first six years after graduating from university – much less pronounced. Here could still 55% the scientist and 77% of their female colleagues realize a career together with their partners, and in only every third couple was given priority *to their career.* In total failed with twice as many female scientists from the sixth Year after graduating from university, the dual career as a couple at *her* Career in the Comparison to her male Colleagues.

But what characterizes couples who have a double career and the necessary nimble but more difficult careers for women to were able to compete with the unsuccessful couples? With regard to the labor participation is out of the findings from Chapter 5 Interesting, that Women scientists who have had a double-earner arrangement for a long time accomplished have, *first* no higher Career- and dual career chance than women with interruptions and that they still *second* not the same career opportunities How her male colleagues had. To it becomes two things clearly. dual careers in academic partnerships of women do not fail because of children if the partners and care arrangement find, that her a re-entry ensures
if also (first) with one reduced Working hours. For the others point However, these findings also indicate that intra-partnership interdependencies arrangements external career barriers for scientists only can partially compensate. However, they are by no means irrelevant, because for the partnerships of the scientists shows that the low better career opportunities for their women through a traditional prioritizing his career through a single-earner or single-career arrangement ment is caused – that children, however, for this traditional division of labor no role played.

Are children meaningless for your career? No, they are not. However, the above findings make it clear that women in science, on the one hand, less frequently than their male counterparts, even without children colleagues a career or together with their partners a double career succeeds. On the other hand, there is the question of career breaks and their Duration is key. With that comes not children per se, but attaches particular importance to the respective *care arrangements , such as* Chapter 3 shows. A career could women with children especially then realize if they - in view of the very widespread use of a traditional nell division of labour between the both partners – already in the first Age of the child External care facilities in combination with Use support services provided by private third parties. This early timely and flexible externalization enabled them to The beginning, tied together with one bigger flexibility regarding the daily Working hours, as they do not match the opening hours of the care facilities were bound, but at the same time also through the use of the care facilities directions did not overwhelm their networks. Furthermore, a par-continued work during (short) parental leave as a condition for success tion, which results in continuous integration into professional networks lightened (please refer Section 1.3). succeeded this not, duration one clearly higher risk of a career break or even termination.

–   This leaves the question unanswered as to why not all academics couples followed this care arrangement.

What were the beneficial ones Conditions for the realization of such an arrangement? For shows Chapter 3 first, that it not at *motivational differences* lay. Women with children were even more likely to have a career in *science* than women without children (77% vs. 63%). Nevertheless, it can be observed that successful but childless women for this goal more often their desire to have children yet hadn't realized, but also didn't want to do without children in general ten. differences in the career orientations the Women were with it not from the desire to have children rather before everything – How Chapter 4 shows – through their experiences with the external framework more scientifically careers and the professional situation in the couple. There is first to hold on that the professional situation the male partner in the rule was safer than that of women (for an explanation see the explanation ments in section 1.3, individual level). Against the background of this same Experience *in the Pair* as well as of their respective own Experiences with

"Linked Lives" in Science

Female scientists also have fixed-term contracts or unemployment on the one hand, the male professional ethos of science (see section 1.2) internalized and on the other hand measure only on the basis of these experiences - and not qua gender - the problem of reconciling work and family a higher priority than their husbands and male colleagues. *successful* scientists develop included very different professional orientations that help them deal with this compatibility problem: Some of them give up the individual persecution ing the career goals of both partners over the family other part, on the other hand, hold an equal family orientation right. For the latter, the "vocation to science" goes beyond the content, not advancement, and remaining in academia is dependent on the opportunities more flexible working conditions dependent made. The Career- However, the success of these scientists is dependent on the partnership assertive, because he needs the support of the man through an in from a professional point of view, an egalitarian couple relationship and a secure one occupation or a good income of the man.

Central to which care arrangement was practiced in

the couple de, were not motivational situations, but the *support strategies of the Couples and their underlying gender ideas* with regard to lich maternity and paternity of the two Partner. Figure 1.3 shows this the three main patterns observed in the analyzes of Chapter 3 could become. It is striking that, firstly, traditional ideas of equality ments in couples with greater externalization of childcare and not - as many would have expected - go hand in hand with a lower one can. Secondly must egalitarian notions of equality the Women, if she not on same to you egalitarian imaginations at your partners encounter, do not lead to such greater externalization. This However, women then run the risk of taking the main job against their will. take on the responsibility and main burden of looking after the children – without help and experience career restrictions as a result.

This is not the place to detail these three patterns, or to to explain how they came about (see Chapter 3 in this book). It is important at this point, with regard to the balancing of the realization conditions of scientific careers for women and double to emphasize that traditional notions of division of labor in childcare *does not* match traditional career aspirations women must go along; nevertheless it is important that women stick to adhere to perceiving both partners as *equals at work* , so that this woman en then seek external support and continue their careers (see Group 1 in Figure 1.3).

* Mention of the discipline groups in which this pattern was most common Source: compilation from findings out of Chapter 3 in this A book

Conversely, women's right to equality in childcare ung, which encounters a traditional role model of the man, to a subsequent involvement of "third parties". The claim to equality Partner is maintained for (too) long.

Legitimacy strate- gies developed on the part of these women to explain why their partner *can* no longer do (e.g. traditional gender role assumptions on the part of the employer for the male partner anti- cipated); but even these and the conflictual disputes about the lack of participation of the partner in the couple (in which also the traditional the partner's attitude becomes visible, since despite this explicit th negotiation processes in the couple not involved) do not lead to that this Women early after external Support or. discharge seek.

Regarding professional continuity after the birth of children as well as the success of the external support in their care shows Kap- tel 3 that they could be managed better with "only" one child. Professionally successful mothers were more likely to have only one child (48% vs. 74% of mothers without a career). Beyond the care arrangement – but definitely also as a favorable factor for the use of external ones support services – is also the *time of the birth of the child* significant. Female scientists who raise their children after their PhD received and/or from a successful career then more likely to continue their careers than women who start at a rather early age point in time in their scientific career have had their children or at a time when they were unsuccessful in their careers. essential che factors for this Advantages of later timings are differences in the financial resources for (flexible) external Care, in the career

"Linked Lives" in Science

resources *of both* partners, in the assumptions of motivation on the part of the donors and colleagues as well as in the possibilities of continuation or reconnection at already established professional networks. For Men starting a family has (so far) had no impact on career reopportunities - not even if they are with a scientist (with a career) living together.

These findings should by no means be understood as

a plea for this that young women and their partners strategically planning and relocating to the back and that thus necessarily taking precedence over the demands of the professional sphere due. However, they make it clear that the external care options ten and the couple's internal care strategies are of particular importance when realizing a career with a child – and can therefore also be seen as an indication of changes that would be necessary about the relationship between career opportunities for women and family establishment and its timing (see below). This would be too therefore worthwhile because the question of the right point in time – which many of the interviewed academic couples in the did place – for many from them emotionalnal is very distressing.

How important are *spatial mobility* and *living arrangements* in academic partnerships? Chapter 5 shows that only 60% of the academically homogeneous and 66% of the occupational field heterogeneous double couples lived in the same place. But also with scientists unemployed partners it was only 70%. multilocal residential arrangements are therefore (at least temporarily) for many scientific students to everyday family life. But they are not a success factor for one per se dual career. For example, the analyzes in Chapter 5 showed that that in scientifically homogeneous couples female scientists with multilo-Kalen housing arrangements did not have a higher double career chance than theirs Colleagues who lived with their partner in one place. More important than that living arrangement was much more the Ask, whether the employer in the course of the professional biography was changed, because given the career patterns in science involves spatial stability with a significant reduction the chance of realizing individual and thus dual careers at scientists along. The is called, the Reside at separate places,the not through Change of

employer is caused does not contribute to career at. Conversely, the strategic approach to employer and thus increases career-related job changes that both partners may have to move to one location can lead to the likelihood that the couple will receive a double card re succeed. Here shows itself in turn: Both – external career conditions on the local labor markets tied together with pair internal career strategies
– carries contribute to a higher chance of dual careers realize.

The synopsis of these findings shows that even with academic partnerships ensure professional equality for men and women in form of dual careers is by no means the rule and, moreover, *none* sufficient Condition for one equality the genders in the division of labor within the family. Conversely, an egalitarian relationship arrangement with regard to work and family in the partnership is not sufficient necessary condition for gender equality in the workplace market.

Dual careers are promoted by egalitarian or individualistic couple relationships draws – with those one too fast traditional prioritization the male career through male standardized external conditions professional careers prevented become can – that is rather possible, but not necessarily enforceable. Responsible for this are institutional gender roles and "individualistic" professional cardinal reciprocal patterns that "conflictingly" intersect in the partnership. The Ver- braid from life courses to dual careers is with it more as only a question of logistics or the intra-partnership coordination of institutional claims.

nevertheless should the intra-partnership perspective not under- be appreciated – and not by the couples either. An important prerequisite for the realization of dual careers is the reflected corridor with career patterns and childcare as well as with the deconstruction of gender role ideas outside and within partnership couple - and thus an appropriate assessment of the respective situation. This is important, on the one hand, to avoid inequalities in career opportunities in the couple to recognize and on the other hand at Requirement Possibilities the elimination to explore.

However, Figure 1.4 shows a large discrepancy in this respect: Both scientists clearly overestimate the realization of a dual career in their partnership. Subjective is the vast majority of them believe that they have a double Career leads; real are it but in everyone career stages clearly fewer. As a result, the pressure of the problem is not recognized in many of these partnerships and the barriers to women's careers (because, as explained above, tern the - objective - dual careers mostly on their careers) not actively encountered. Carrying on like this, however, leads to a solidification of the equals in the Pair.

Particularly noticeable is the discrepancy in the scientific workers (with one Difference from 41 percentage points), at those the last career step to the professorship is still pending, which in view of the mostly missing objectively achieved career with this false perception will probably not be easier or more likely. Furthermore, lich, that scientist in everyone career stages more often one distorted

"Linked Lives" in Science

Perception of the realization of a dual career in their partnership have than their female colleagues - and also justified by ten(er) need for action with regard to the professional career opportunities of their see women. Both men and women show that *double earnings ner* arrangements too frequently already with *dual careers* equated be – an equation that, however, like the analyzes in this book show with contributing to the fact that women have fewer careers in science can do).

Contrasts between the objective presence of Double professions and the abstract appraisal

Source: record "Together Profession make"; own estimations

So in the event that we at long last ask what should be possible , our own show Discoveries that further develop vocation open doors for ladies in the Science and related double professions both reasonable outer structure conditions in the expert world as well as expanded reflection, Exchange and coordination administrations expected in the organization are. An expert profession for the two accomplices - with concurrent It is hence important to empower upkeep of organization and, if fundamental, life as a parent more adaptable work associations, with those likewise the Necessities the family can be accommodated; it requires greater adaptability and with the functioning scene tuned outer kid care offices (in any case contingent upon the particular wallets of the couples) as well as changed models in Connection on Orientation and Vocation in the Organization as well as additionally in the association self. minds what's more, How this look could, have formed in an autonomous activity pamphlet (cf. Hess/Rusconi/Solga 2011b).

2.   interweaving arrangements in the pair history

2.1 The interweaving of career paths in couples between structural conditions and adaptive strategies

Object this chapter is the study of interdependence patterns of employment histories in pairs, i.e. the combination of (employment) shares viabilities of the two partners, and the question of whether certain professional and family liary events lead to changes in the interconnectedness. The term The interweaving pattern is intended to make it clear that the combination is not selectively - i.e. only at a single point in time (e.g. month or year) -, but took place in long-term phases of life or characterized them. [1] As discussed in the previous chapter, an essential requirement for dual careers, that both partner one occupation pursue. Then especially with these so-called double-income couples, over- ask the question to what extent both partners were able to to achieve a professional position that is appropriate to their respective education and their institutional age was.

Intertwining patterns in pairs are the result of the interaction of gender specific processes on different levels (for one Discussion see Rusconi/Solga 2008; Rusconi/Solga 2010). on the social social, cultural and institutional frameworks influence conditions – such as B. gender-specific segregation processes in education and on the labor market or job-specific work culture and career logics, but also the social expectations of them Organization of care for relatives (especially children) – who integration possibilities from Women and men in partnerships. As illustrated in the term " *family adaptive strategy* ", family en and their members, however, do not simply passively follow institutional guidelines and framework conditions. Rather, couples work on and process these specifications ben and can adaptive strategies develop, with those she attempt,

---

1   im following becomes alternatively also the Expression arrangement used her professional and private Goals to to reach (see. Moen/Wethington 1992). "The concept of strategy calls forth the active (rather than the passive) role of the family unity and underscores the dynamic nature of family life; families mobilize and modify their plan other behavior like their circumstances change." (Moen/Wethington 1992: 246) Find such processes on the extra- and intra-partnership level not in a juxtaposition, but in a reciprocal relationship connection to one another (cf. Geissler/Oechsle 2001; Moen/Wethington 1992). Changes in the framework conditions can lead to adjustments in the interweaving, and changes in strategy can in turn change the (relative) position one or both partners on the labor market and thus the opportunity entity structures for particular interweaving arrangements postpone. In addition, strategies can evolve over the course of the partnership changes in the Tasks, priorities and Requirements, but also in the goals of one or both partners at the various stages of relationships and individual careers (cf. Levy/Ernst 2002; Monday 2003; Nock 1998).

, the empirically found patterns of interdependence are *neither* partnership strategies *nor* as the sum of decisions of the to understand individual family members. First of all, because they result of the interplay of intra-partnership decisions – including (explicit or tacit) compromises and agreements between the partners - with the non-partnership framework represent things. This means that interweaving patterns can also be the desired result of partnership strategies, if e.g. B. after a as temporal limited conceived career break the re-entry unsuccessful in the job. And secondly, because power relations between family members (see. Blood/Wolfe 1960), often stratified through Old and gender (see Saraceno 1989), the processes of decision-making. influence significantly, so that the family or couple strategies do not (must) correspond to the wishes and interests of both partners (cf. the chapter 3 and 5 in this A book).

Research questions of this chapter are which interweaving patterns of the Employment trajectories are practicing scientists and what dynamics they are subject to through certain professional and family Events? To what extent and with whom is it only temporary changes or to long-term "changes"?

Entanglement arrangements in the course of the pair

2.2 *interweaving pattern and "Exercise Points"*

This chapter will take a life-course perspective that will allow possible, structural aspects as well as individual and intra-partnership Factors in a temporal (historical, but also biographical) context menhang to bring (see. Kohli 1985). Also taken into account such one perspective also the Ask after to the Influence earlier life events,

-conditions and decisions for the further life course (see. Mayer 1991). The focus of this chapter is on the dynamics of the patterns of the employment trajectories of scientists and their partners ner above the career cycle on the one hand and above the family cycle on the other hand. Because changes in both spheres can present couples with new ones pose challenges, but also open up new options for them, which new interweaving patterns to lead (see. Levy/Ernst 2002; moen 2003; Nock 1998). The distinction between professional and family spheres is to be understood only as an analytical separation, because in reality Men and Women contemporaneous in specific professional and family phases,

e.g. B. in the doctoral phase and at the same time mother or father of a child of.

In the *professional sphere* , employment in science manages the qualification phases centrally. For a career at a high school or non-university research institution, the doctorate is few exceptions essential. The acquisition of the doctorate also marks the one central step in the professional development of management forces in public administration, politics and the private sector and provides with it also here a important factor at the climb the career ladder (cf. Enders/Bornmann 2001; Hartmann 2002). The possibility Taking on responsible (management) tasks often goes hand in hand hand with the acquisition of the

doctorate. In addition, form of employment and scope of work for Activities, the one promotion assume for example in science: apart from some disciplines and gender differences become after the promotion Grants are less common and full-time employment contracts are more common (cf. Hess/Rusconi/ Solga 2011a; Zimmer/Krimmer/Stallmann 2007). Regarding the financial protection and job and career opportunities makes a pro motion has a positive effect in many professional areas. The associated which increased financial resources enable couples on the one hand rather individualistic models of the interdependence of their employment trajectories practice (cf. Bathmann/Müller/Cornelißen 2011; Dettmer/Hoff 2005), because this means, for example, separate residences, commuting, but also external ones Childcare solutions are more affordable - which means that both parties able to carry out their gainful employment relatively independently of each other. on the other hand open she couples also the Possibility, on one (second) Refrain from gainful employment, especially if in addition to financial resources the professional Requirements after the promotion also have risen and couples before (In)compatibility problems be asked.
With the takeover from managerial duties is the task often not more
"only" the Write the own qualification work and possibly. the cooperation on a project, but also the acquisition and implementation of a project project and the guidance of employees. It is therefore a matter of gifts, the with bigger spatial-temporal availability requirements can go hand in hand. In addition, the requirements often increase spatial mobile to be to advance your own career.

One Investigation PhD scientists and engineeringrun within and outside of the Science could show, that after the doctorate, the first four years of professional establishment are the most mobile Phase represent and that a positive relationship between moves and professional success (Becker et al. 2011: 42f.). Especially women with management positions (from middle management) were often mobile male than their female colleagues in lower professional positions (Becker et al. 2011: 42). A study on work-related illnesses came to similar conclusions mobility from academic and not academic educated persons in Germany: Mobile are before everything persons with leading position in the middle management. On the other hand, the job-related relocation and commuting mobility in the higher career stages away (Cutter et al. 2008: 134). These forms of mobility are therefore for climbing the career ladder necessary. However, once a top position has been reached, either the mobile quality requirements lower or the Possibilities greater, itself this Requirements to oppose (cf. Schneider et al. 2008). Over and beyond the relocation mobility is above average for people who are temporary are busy; i.e. occupational insecurity also increases the need thing spatial mobility (Schneider et al. 2008: 135).

Due to long qualification phases in typically temporary employment relationships are precisely career paths in science compared to other professional fields due to a longer phase of insecurity safety marked. First the vocation on lifetime (Professorship) in a comparatively late phase of life represents a secure (unlimited) employment (cf. Zimmer/Krimmer/Stallmann 2007). career paths in the Science are not only comparatively long, rather also very risky, then one professorship obtained loud estimates from jason, Schomburg and Teichler (2006: 70, 72) only every tenth doctorate and every third "serious candidate". Accordingly, university careers will also as particularly "precarious careers" (cf. Enders 2003).

Professional tasks and requirements, but also time

and financial cial possibilities differ before and after the doctorate. From therefore puts itself the Ask, in what way this both career phases with

Intertwining arrangements in the course of the pair

different interweaving patterns the employment histories the Knowledge- employees and their partners. Will the increased spatial-temporal job requirements in the postdoc phase with one increase from single-earner partnerships accompanied? Consist given the higher uncertainty scientific careers scientifically On the one hand, partnerships are more likely to be made up of double-income couples, but they on the other hand particularly "unstable" interweaving pattern represent, there in In these couples, both partners work in the "risky" professional field of science are?

From a large number of studies it is known that in the *private sphere* the birth of the first child leads to adjustments in the patterns of interdependence of employment can lead to partnerships (cf. e.g. Becker/Moen 1999; Small 1996; Schulz/Blossfeld 2006). Straight the social Expectations of spatial-temporal availability and responsibility of the mother for her child(ren) is often at odds with professional chen requirements (Hardill/van Loon 2007: 169) and often leads to Employment interruptions and career (departure) breaks (cf. Chapter 3 in this A book; Genen 1993; Vogel/Hinz 2003). Fathers, on the other hand, aiming to secure the family and thus professional advancement, But not (yet) their spatial and temporal availability for the family (cf. Hardill/Van Loon 2007). The intertwining of life and work run in partnerships so wins at Complexity, if from couples become families (cf. Hess/Rusconi/Solga 2011a), especially since the temporal and spatial demands on the professional and private sphere completely different logics results, while perhaps not even inverse are. It is notable that ladies are almost certain than men after the introduction of their first of intruding on their profitable work, however which job do the interlace design before birth? In which couples are just momentarily momentary changes, and which are long haul changes? lungs - and why?

These inquiries are talked about underneath along the logical split among work and family stage was inspected. While in Area 2.3 the techniques and definitions shown become, is Segment 2.4 the Devoted to examination of reliance designs when doctoral examinations and Segment 2.5 the joining designs the introduction of first kid.

2.3   *methods and definitions*

The data with the scientists serve as the basis for this chapter conducted standardized life course interviews (see Chapter 1 in this sem A book). As first career phase becomes the PhD phase examined.

This phase is called the three years for scientists with a doctorate defined before acquiring a doctorate, while scientists the at the time of interviews still did not have a doctorate the three years before the interview were considered. [2] For the phase after the promotion tion, all scientists with a doctorate (incl. professors with doctorate) included in the analysis and their interdependence patterns up to examined up to six years after the acquisition of this qualification. For the Comparison of the interdependence patterns in the course of the family, all knowledge involved with at least one biological child in the analysis genes observed at least two years before the birth of the first child became. As "most intense" family phase became the interweaving patterns up to six years after birth of the first child considered.

About the question of the dynamic interdependence of employment histories to pursue in partnerships, was for each month of the respective career or family phase, whether the scientists were involved in a partnership at all. [3] lay a partnership before, each month was combining the activity of the two partners considered and between the presence or absence of distinguish between two jobs. [4] If you only have one job in Two categories were formed: [5]

– earner: Only the partner/the partner went one occupationafter.

– sole earner: Only the scientist was employed.

In the case of interdependencies with two jobs, the combination nations of the professional fields of the activities of the two partners three categories certainly:

- science homogenous dual earner: Both partner were in the sciencescience system employed.

---

2 Scientists with a shorter observation period were excluded from the analysis excluded, which affected16% of the scientists (mainly at the time of interviews non-doctoral students).

3 For both professional and family phases became scientists out of the analysis excluded those who were with more than one partner. This came rarely found in our sample: Only 6% of the scientists had more than one part- nership in the three years before the doctorate and 6% during the six years after the doctorate Promotion. Only four male and two female scientists lived in more than one Partnership in the two years before the birth of their first child. all science students stayed in the same partnership in the six years thereafter.

4 grants with one financial Financial support become as gainful employment considered.

5 Strictly speaking, both categories are single-earner couples, since only one partner is employed. The conceptual distinction between the categories of single and earner only serves to distinguish who was employed in the partnership: part- ner or Scientist.

Entanglement arrangements in the course of the pair

- Occupational field heterogeneous double earners: The scientists were within, the partners outside of science occupied.

- double earner outside of the Science: Both partner went He-commercial activities outside of science after. Finally, all those couples in which both partners were not employed.

Since this chapter deals with the interdependence in certain professional and family lien phases and not just at a single point in time (e.g. month or year), the exploratory tive method of "optimal matching" for sequence analysis (cf. Brzinsky-Fay/Kohler/Luniak 2006). For the respective professional or family lien phases were combining the activities of the two partners for determined each month (see above) and in their chronological order sequence to sequences composed. This sequences became then compared to create a distance matrix, [6] which the formed the starting point for the cluster analysis. With her then groups of Sequences – ie researchers with similar sequences of braid – identified. [7] The homogeneity within the clusters and the Heterogeneity between the clusters made it possible to classify the content of the (existing) interconnectedness characteristic of these phases pattern.

Along the analytical separation between professional and family phase the following section first examines descriptively which braid pattern the scientists before and after the promotion practiced and the dynamics of this during the two professional phases subject. Then, using multivariate analyses, the influence occupational structural, origin and couple characteristics for certain relationships interweaving patterns are examined and the significance of earlier interweaving rangements explored on later. For this purpose, in section 2.4.3 hypotheses well formulated. With the same structure, in section 2.5 the braid pattern after birth of the first child examined.

---

[6] As is usual in research, the costs for substitutions were taken into account to 2, the indel cost (insertion and deletion) set to 1 (cf. Brzinsky-Fay/Kohler/ luniak 2006).

7   The Ward method (hierarchical method) was used here. There, however conventional statistical tests are not applicable with sequence data, the final number of clusters due to differences in content - as well as sufficient case numbers - is correct (Brzinsky-Fay 2007: 413).

2.4 Interdependence arrangements in the course of work

2.4.1 Pattern the interweaving

The analysis of the interdependence of the career paths of scientists and their partners in the three years before the doctorate makes six Pattern (Figure 2.1).

Figure 2.1: Intertwining pattern of employment histories before doctoratethe Scientists *
dv = double earner
All scientists the at least three observed years before graduation became. In the case of non-doctoral students, this is the period three years before Interview.
Source: record "Together Career make"; own calculations

The most common arrangement were occupational field heterogeneous double earner (31%, pattern #2), [8] ie pairs in which the scientists had employment in the scientific field while the partners one employment in one others professional field pursued. The second

---

[8] quantitative descriptions became regarding of gender, the career level and Disciplines are weighted so that - as provided for in the sampling plan (cf. Chapter 1 in this A book) – always to same shares represent are.

Intertwining arrangements in the course of the pair

most common groups were for the a single earner arrangements, so Couples where only the scientist is looking for a job went (24%, pattern no. 4), and on the other hand scientifically homogeneous double earners (23%, pattern #1), ie couples where both partners are in the Science employed were. Also because of ours sampling was only a minority of scientists in the doctoral phase predominantly single (11%, sample #6). [9] Also very rare were arrangements in which only the partner seeks employment went (7%, pattern #5), as well as dual earner arrangements outside of the Academic, ie couples where both partners are not in college or. in the scientific field (3%, sample No. 3).

The distribution this six interweaving pattern differs itself clearly between genders and career stages. [10] Already in the doctoral phase, there were three main differences between knowledge learn and scientists. *First* : The three dual earner arrangements together were the most common interweaving of both sexes ter. However, they were more common among female scientists than theirs Colleagues (66% vs. 50%, Figure 2.2). About a third of males Prior to his doctorate, the scientist was the sole breadwinner in the partner community, while only a minority of women did (35% vs. 13%). *Secondly* gives it a clear gender difference in the Dissemination of scientifically homogeneous partnerships. At almost one third of female scientists, but less than a fifth of them male colleagues, both partners were active in science (29% vs. 17%). *Third* , more than twice as many women scientists practiced like scientists the single earner arrangement (10% vs. 3.5%). Mean- However, differences were evident in the spread of heterogeneous to partnerships as well as from the single pattern and from dual earner arrangements outside of science.

9   Due to random sampling, none of the data at the time of the interview belonged to this pattern non-doctoral students (see Chapter 1 in this book). This group included 23% of the at the time of the interview male and female postdocs and 13% of the professors sors and 15% of female professors.

10 There are also differences between disciplines, which are not descriptively mentioned for reasons of space will be dealt with in more detail. It should only be briefly pointed out here that men like Homogenous partnerships were more common among women in the natural sciences than in the other disciplines (cf. Hess/Rusconi/Solga 2011a). Almost 40% of natural science women and at least one-fifth of their specialist colleagues were part of a research scientist couple. For women of the other disciplines, however, this arrangement is no exception either: 27% of technical and 22% of social science belonged to the academically homogeneous group. In the technical and social sciences scientists were it 15% or. 16.5%.

Source: record "Together Career make"; own calculations; weighted Declarations

In summary, it becomes clear that more female scientists than senschaftler confronted with the challenge even before the doctorate are, two gainful employment in the common layout from Profession and family to consider. In addition, this interdependence takes place at Women held it much more often than their male counterparts in the same Occupational field (ie in science). Because of a "shared knowledge" and "mutual understanding" of the rules, requirements and Possibilities of shaping the common profession can such a support for the professional development of both parties ner (cf. Hess/Rusconi/Solga 2011a). Since in academic n partnerships, however, both partners are comparatively risky and pursue an uncertain career, such a match can also bring additional stress and risk of failure. With These "advantages and disadvantages" are female scientists more often than schaftler confronted.

The comparison of the interdependence patterns between scientists, who were at different career stages at the time of the interview found, however, makes it clear that this also applies to male scientists Dual Earner Partnerships in the PhD phase increasingly the Rule become. So register the three dual earner arrangements to- together a clear Increase of 37% among today's professors 50% for postdocs and even 68% for those who have not (yet) graduated. In the In return, there was "only" almost a third of the male non-doctoral students and postdocs are the sole breadwinners in the partnership while this is on almost half of the professors were correct (46%). Furthermore, it turns out that in particular scientifically homogeneous partnerships as interweaving pattern at significance

Intertwining arrangements in the course of the pair

win. Almost a third of the male non-doctoral graduates, but only just under a fifth of male postdocs and 6% of professors ren in the doctoral phase one academically homogeneous partnership. [11]

Because of this marked increase in dual earner patterns across common and the scientifically homogeneous pattern in particular young male and female scientists in similar partnerships. Have female scientists always been confronted with the challenge ted to combine two career paths even before the doctorate weave, is this one Task, the nowadays also increasingly on theirs male colleagues (cf. Chapter 1 in this A book).

2.4.2 *dynamics the interweaving pattern*

The entwining of vocation ways in associations is because of changes portrayed. From one viewpoint, while prevailing in all examples - as in Figure 2.1 shown - obviously a mix of the exercises of the two the accomplice, however there are likewise researchers in each example, who on occasion practice an alternate blend of their expert exercises embellished. Then again, relationship designs likewise shift over the direction of a profession. The interlacing the work accounts the for the hour of meetings graduated researchers and teachers for the Period as long as six years after the doctorate shows the two likenesses and furthermore contrasts contrasted with the courses of action before the doctorate (Figure 2.3). After the doctorate there were five gatherings, each with a somewhat unique dispersion to match designs during advancement. 12 Moreover is there one further Gathering, the straight through one blend various mixes of the exercises of the two accomplices draws is (design #6). 13

11 With regard to the spread of academically homogeneous and sole In terms of earnings, there are only minor differences of no more than 5 percentage points. Both Female scientists is the biggest difference between the career levels in the Dissemination of occupational field heterogeneous arrangements: Their proportion falls from 39% among non- received their doctorates at 23% among today's female professors. This difference is mostly due to the higher proportion of female professors who gles were.

12 As before the doctorate, about half of the scientists carry out a vocational rogen (31%, pattern no. 2) or academically homogeneous dual-income partnership

(21%, pattern #1). Single earners (12%, Pattern #4) and dual earner arrangements outside of academia (5%, pattern #3). There is also a single group significantly less frequently after the doctorate (4%, pattern #5). After the doctorate, however, there is no clear single-earner arrangement from one non-employment of the Scientist.

One further subdivision this pattern brings two further groups to appear (not illustrated). On the one hand, a combination of occupational field heterogeneous double earnings call and single earner arrangements, at those the partner not employed was. dv = double earner

* graduated scientists (Incl. professors)

Source: record "Together Career make"; own calculations.

An examination of the gathering participation when the doctorate shows both long-lasting game plans and changes. From the information and researchers who have an expert field before their doctorate heterogeneous organization had, heard something less as the a portion of the Men and something else as the a portion of the Ladies likewise in the accompanying six years this gathering at (47% versus 54%). more clear contrasts among people, nonetheless, exist among the individuals who changed meshing design after graduation. While 17% of Scholastics who had an expertly heterogeneous accomplice prior to doing their doctorate were the sole provider subsequent to finishing their doctorate, there were a change at none Researcher. Only on extremely rare occasions saw as an expert

On the other hand, a combination of occupationally heterogeneous double earners and agreement service arrangements where the scientist was not employed.

The first Combination is more common among male than female scientists (17.5% vs. 10%), while the Opposite at the second combination the case is (6% vs. 18%).Since these groups have many censored cases (i.e. the interview took place earlier than six years after the doctorate) is discussed in the following explanations and analyses this groups not closer received.

Entanglement arrangements in the course of the pair

field change – in the senses one Recording from activities in the Science

– of partners (less than 4% of both men and women). [14] One similar height stability the interweaving pattern was at Science- to find students who, before completing their doctorate, worked in communities: 52% of men and 57% of women did so in the following six years. At this group gave it however also ge bad type change the Interweaving Pattern: After the promotion became 17% the Scientist, but only one scientist for the sole earner. Another 13% of women, but only 3% of men change to the occupational field-heterogeneous double earner arrangement, i.e. their partners ner were not more in science system employed. [15]

So scientists weren't only half leading even before they got their doctorate as often a scientifically homogeneous partnership as their colleagues, but Others also remained somewhat less frequently with this arrangement Course. same is applicable for occupational field heterogeneous Partnerships: Fewer Scientists as scientists lived permanently in such a place Arrangement. Stability, on the other hand, is evident for male scientists in the single-earner pattern: 42% of them remained after the pattern motion with this arrangement (vs. 14% of scientists), and only one third of the scientists switched to one of the three dual nerpattern. For the women in this group, on the other hand, it was 29% their partners, who were not previously gainfully employed, take up a job in science and for another 14% the partners were found outside of science shaft employed.

Compared to the doctoral phase, the postdoc phase is composed of to summarize that the proliferation of dual earner partnership increased slightly (from 55% to

58% of those with doctorates and professors sors). On the one hand, this development was caused by the fact that Majority of scientists who completed their doctorate in the single group belonged after the promotion Part one double earner couple became (52% of the scientists and 65% of the scientists in this group). On the other hand, a third of the male scientists who worked before were the sole earner of the doctorate, to one of the three double earner groups. This "late" Recording one employment on the part the partner is also associated with the characteristic age difference in couples owes: Because female partners are typically younger than the scientific ler (see Chapter 1 in this book) so that they can be used at a later date her Studies graduate and get a job to record.

---

14 About 30% of the scientists from the previously heterogeneous group switched to the mixed group. Admittedly, such a change was more common among women than men find, the gender difference is however with only 5 percentage points very small amount.

15 About another fifth of the scientists of the previously scientifically homogeneous group changed to the mixed Group. Here exists no gender difference.

Nevertheless, male scientists were and remained not only tener in double earner arrangements than their female colleagues; also went to them a change in the interweaving pattern much more frequently with a interruption of their partners' professional activities. If knowledge female scientists, on the other hand, left a dual earner pattern, then before everything because of one change in the field of activity of partners (before everything in scientifically homogeneous partnerships). That means in all professional sen, the gainful employment of female scientists takes place predominantly in context of a dual earner partnership.

These couples ought to however from one perspective have the potential for double vocations (see Sections 1 and 5 in this book); then again, they are confronted with the extra difficulties gen confronted, the two positions for joint preparation and design from Calling and Family address. That the Adapting of these difficulties is a troublesome undertaking to which accomplice organizations frequently with a (impermanent) renunciation of productive work of the accomplices in responded becomes, show the Outcomes for the entwining design the male Researcher.

2.4.3 *Between approximation and persevere differed*

In the previous finishes became differences in the intertwining tion patterns the scientists and scientist clearly. In the The following examines the reasons why a certain entanglement arrangement was practiced and whether the gender difference through a gender-specific effect of the same characteristics and/or something like that so-called composition effects (ie a different group composition setting regarding certain characteristics) explain can let.

On the one hand, *occupational structure characteristics are used as explanatory factors* taken into account: the discipline of the first academic degree and the graduating cohort. Especially since the beginning of the 1990s, the participation rate of academically educated women has risen sharply (cf. Anger/Konegen-Gre- ner 2008). This should reduce the likelihood of dual earner partner sciences – both among male scientists and in science shank – favor. Accordingly, the gender differences should Scientists who have obtained their first academic degree since 1990 acquired may be lower than in the older graduating cohort. Nonetheless must taken into account become, that Women in typical male disciplines were and will remain disadvantaged in their employment opportunities (cf. Solga/ Pfahl 2009), which is a higher risk of (involuntary) career breaks and consequently ge One-earner arrangements could result.

Furthermore, *characteristics of origin are* taken into account: the place of birth in West- or East Germany and the employment the Mother while

Intertwining arrangements in the course of the pair

your own childhood. Not only before the "Wende" but also today the two parts of Germany differ significantly in terms of one Acceptance of and support for women's employment (cf. Dressel 2005) – an important prerequisite for realizing double earnings arrangements. Accordingly, the difference in the interconnection tern between west german scientists and scientists be larger than their East German colleagues. Similarly, should- ten a "more egalitarian" socialization and the role model of the employed mother the probability of sex-typical single or single reduce earning arrangements for both men and women. This should to lesser differed between scientists and scientists with working mothers to lead.

Finally become *sociodemographic pair traits* taken into account: the age constellation and the presence of children. previous company searches to the Significance of age constellation for employment arrangements in pairs of academics show – albeit not unequivocally – that double Servant arrangements are more enforceable when women are older than their partners (cf. Rusconi/Solga 2007; Solga/Rusconi/Krüger 2005). About it In addition, it is to be expected that partners of the same age will primarily have the opportunity for scientifically homogeneous Pattern restrict could. At this couples certain (and similar) career steps and requirements must be time- be mastered equally, while couples from heterogeneous occupations different professional logics at least partially an equalization of the requirements can support. Finally, it is known from the literature that children increase the risk of gender-typical single-earner arrangements hen (see section 2.2 as well as Chapter 3 in this book). Therefore should the differences between male and female scientists children be bigger than between childless individuals.

In the accompanying, it will be analyzed what impact word related construction, future and match attributes on the connection of specific entrapment bunches had for the time before the doctorate. As displayed in segment 2.4.1 there are clear contrasts among guys and females Researchers in the spread of the sole worker and single worker game plans as well as the experimentally homogeneous double worker design. The likelihood of having a place with one of these gatherings was determined utilizing inspected by direct likelihood relapses. The overall tive probabilities of female researchers contrasted with male senschaftlern: The worth 1 implies that people are a similar Likelihood for a particular intertwining design, values more prominent than 1 sign a higher likelihood for females, and on the other hand, esteems under 1 have a lower likelihood. as arbitrator The reference classification for the relationship design became heterogeneous in the word related field course of action picked, ie couples, at those the Researcher at

was utilized at a college or examination foundation during the accomplice sought after a calling beyond science. As in the examined in the past areas, this was the most well-known ter for male and female researchers and the gathering with the least distinction in sexual orientation.

Figure 2.4: Relative probability of women compared to men for single, single-earner and academic homo-genes pattern before the doctorate (reference: berufsfeldhete-rogen pattern)

M0 : sex; *M1* : job structure characteristics; *M2* : job structure + origin characteristics; *M3* : occupational structure + origin characteristics + pair traits
Source: record "Together Career make"; own calculations

Figure 2.4 shows the relative probabilities of science compared to scientists, the sole breadwinner, Single-earner or academically homogeneous double-earner arrangement in to belong to the doctoral phase. If no other feature than the poorly considered, scientists are twice as likely to probability of how female scientists are the sole earners in the partner shaft (M0). [16] Conversely, for female scientists there is a more than double probability across from your Colleagues, in one agreement

---

[16] The probability of a single-earner pattern compared to heterogeneous gene dual earner arrangement was 54% (vs. 28% at scientists).

Intertwining arrangements in the course of the pair

to live as a servant (ie only the partner is employed). [17] Men and women, on the other hand, differ only slightly in terms of their probability one scientifically homogeneous dual earnerarran gements compared to an occupational field heterogeneous. With one exception remain this gender differences also after consideration the occupational structure, origin and couple characteristics are relatively unchanged (M1-M3 in Figure 2.4). Only for the single earner pattern will the gender difference smaller; starting with the model that turelle Features considered.

Regarding the *occupational structure characteristics* showed itself on the one hand, that in comparison to occupational field heterogeneous dual earner arrangements in older and younger graduation cohorts the probability for knowledge women to be the sole breadwinner in the partnership, only half so was as large as their peers (Figure 2.5). On the other hand, solvent females in the younger cohort are twice as likely to a single earner arrangement because of one own non-employment respectively. In this respect, graduates differ venten of the older cohort hardly from each other. These findings contradict the expectation of increasing similarity in the partnerships of the younger graduates, because in the cohort comparison the Gender difference in the single-earner model only slightly decreased has increased and has even increased in the case of the single earner pattern. only out of lich of the scientific or non-scientific occupational field Partners there is a clear rapprochement: while men and Women the younger cohort with more similar probability knowledge-community-homogeneous or -heterogeneous dual-income arrangements practiced ten, this was not the case in the older cohort. Compared to one occupational field heterogeneous arrangement were scientists of the older cohort three times more likely than their peers a pair of scientists.

With regard to differences between disciplines, it was shown that social compared to their specialist colleagues (more than double pelt so) had a high risk of a single-earner arrangement due to a to lead own non-employment. Male and female science scientist distinguished itself however not from each other. The relative Probability of women compared to men in the technical sciences cannot be calculated, because although 18% of technical scientists, but none of their male peers this ver

---

17 The probability of a single-earner pattern compared to the occupational field heterogeneous a dual earner arrangement was 24% for female scientists (vs. 10% for female scientists scientists).

Figure 2.5: Relative likelihood of women compared to men for single, single earner and scientific senschafthomogenous pattern before the doctorate according to selected characteristics (reference: occupationalheterogeneous pattern)

Source: record "Together Career make"; own calculations

Entanglement arrangements in the course of the pair

braided pattern. [18] The expectation that technical and natural workers given of their in the Comparison to men worse labor market opportunities a higher probability of (unwanted) income have earning patterns can therefore only be confirmed for the former. A possible explanation for the higher probability of social scientists were, that it in the social sciences in the Comparison to the others disciplines one more precarious professional situation there, e.g. B. with regard to the unemployment rate and time limits on employment sluggish (cf. Diaz-Bone/Glöckner/Küffer 2004). Even if in this discipline plin women experience fewer disadvantages than women in typically male disciplines (cf. Chapter 1 in this book), they are still threatened higher risk of being unemployed than their peers. summary The expectations with regard to the structural characteristics of the occupation could be sent neither fully confirmed still refuted become.

Contrary to the expectation of increasing similarity in the braiding patterns existed for scientists also the youngest graduating cohort different probabilities, Single or single-earner arrangements in an earlier career phase respectively. The increasing opening of the professional field of science - on the lower career levels – for women, however, meant that young scientists male and female scientists with the same probability dual earner arrangement in the same professional field practiced.

Also with regard to the influence of the *characteristics of origin,* the results not ambivalent. With regard to the probability of a single or single-earner pattern in comparison to an occupational field heterogeneous double earnings arrangement is, as expected, the difference between West German cal men and women greatest. West German men were with them one nearly twice higher probability as her female colleagues the sole earner, while West German women, unlike their place a double so high risk for a single earner arrangement had. The differences between East German men and women were gene minimal. The expectation that the employment the own Mother increased the probability of dual earner patterns, however not be confirmed. That the employment of their own mother is not made it more likely that female scientists would be sole breadwinners in occupational field heterogeneous Dual Earner Partnerships lived contrary- does not speak to the expectation of a more "egalitarian" socialization (because in both the women pursue a job). However seem male scientist not in the same Scope benefits from it too have: Because even compared to their male colleagues with non- employed Mother had she one something higher Probability, the

18 Nonetheless is the risk one such arrangements for scientists in the tech engineering lower as in the social sciences.

to be the sole earner. Because of this is the gender difference between scientists with working mothers greater than between those whose mothers were not employed. Also was the parted between this scientists and scientists at the Single-earner pattern larger than for those with an inactive mother- ter. In this case, however, the probability was higher for both women and men with working mothers also slightly less than for their Legs with non-working mothers. The expectation of a favorable ing influence for dual earner arrangements due to an "egalitarian ren" socialization by a working mother can therefore only be however, cannot be unequivocally confirmed for men. This could points out that for intertwining arrangements in partnerships rather from Meaning is, whether the mothers of the women (scientists or female partners) were employed, and less what the mothers of the men (scientist or partner) made have.

With regard to the *couple characteristics* , the age constellation has a significant same influence, especially for single-earner patterns. The biggest difference existed between scientists of the same age gene partnerships. In comparison to a professionally heterogeneous arrangement ment, there was a higher likelihood of men with an age advantage probability for the sole breadwinner pattern as at your Colleagues with partner of the same age, but the same also applied to the (few) female partners with younger partners, so that for this group of difference was very low. Since women, however, much less often than men had an age advantage, 19 may be part of the gender difference in the spread of the single-earner arrangement also on a composite ion effect can be attributed. The expectation is also the Findings: The (few) scientists with older partners were with us less likely than their colleagues with other age constellations tion sole earner. However duration for scientists with older partners an even lower probability, so for this constellation the gender difference remains. These findings confirm that dual earner patterns (here heterogeneous in occupational fields) tend to be in age-atypical partnerships are possible; ie where the women (Partners or scientists) older than their husbands are. But as the term "atypical" already suggests, such (beneficial) Age constellations very rare. For men and women, on the other hand, the The expectation cannot be confirmed that, above all, scientists in peers partnerships with lesser probability knowledge- shaft-homogeneous as occupational field heterogeneous dual earner pattern realized

---

19   On average, scientists were about one year older and women two years younger than their partners (Hess/Rusconi/Solga 2011a: 76). Only 7% of scientists run vs. 53% of their Colleagues had a age advantage from at least one Year.

Entanglement arrangements in the course of the pair

ten. [20] A possible explanation for this finding would be that in this early other professional phase, the simultaneous coping with similar professional requirements was still easy to organize or just as good as in different professional fields. However interpret the Results also thereupon, that thefundamental question in partnerships of the same age is whether two at all

Gainful employment is (can be) realised. Because especially with males Scientists with a partner of the same age is the probability for a single earner arrangement comparatively high. A interweaving pattern, which in these couples of the same age is not explain the partner's delayed entry into the labor market due to age but rather to the difficulties of coping at the same time professional requirements indicates.

Finally, the children should be mentioned. The fact that male Scientists twice as likely as their peers to sole earner were, hung not – at least not to this time

– with the presence of children. Even childless men were more likely to be the sole earners compared to their childless colleagues. In addition, there was no difference between scientists with and without children. [21] On the other hand, for mothers in Twice as likely as fathers to agree servant arrangement because of the own non-employment to to lead, while childless scientists are only here little different from each other. This higher probability or that higher risk of mothers compared to fathers is *not, however* , on it attributed to the fact that mothers are more likely to earn nermuster than childless colleagues had. It was the fathers who compared to their childless colleagues, a substantially lower probability of not being employed themselves. For male Scientists we find so a first indication that fathers of social expectation accordingly the Family through one own secure employment. For women – scientists and partners However, factors other than children seem to play a role for one non-employment to play.

In summary, it can be stated that scientists and scientists scientists gender-typical opportunities for particular intertwining

---

20 For male and female scientists, the probability is one

scientifically homogeneous dual earner arrangements in the Comparison to one professional- field heterogeneity lowest among those younger than their partners. The smallest gender difference was between men and women scientists to with younger to find partners.

21 Not surprisingly, this was also true for women. Compared to a professional field heterogeneous dual earner arrangement was the probability of a single earner arrangement ments for female scientists with and without children approx. 20% (vs. approx. 40% for their male chen Colleagues).

development patterns in the doctoral phase. Especially with regard to the spread of single-earner arrangements compared to professional field-heterogeneous dual earner pattern is the expectation of an increasing the similarity from scientists and scientists clearly refuted been. Only regarding of professional field the Partners foundan approximation takes place in the case of dual-income couples. You can also find Hints on discipline and gender specific risks on to the labor market, i.e. above all with regard to the restrictions on employment activity of social and technical scientists. He also plays social and family context of origin play a significant role. Before especially women (here scientists) benefited from socialization by a working mother in the sense of "sticking" to a employment and in a dual earner pattern. Finally show the results show that dual earner arrangements are more likely to be in partnerships are possible in which the women (partners or scientists to) are older than their husbands.

But to what extent are the interweaving patterns of these see early career phase long term from Meaning, ie for the intertwiningarrangements after graduation?

2.4.4 *Everything at the old or become the cards reshuffled?*

As before the doctorate, the discoveries of multivariate dissects show that that in contrast with the word related field heterogeneous twofold worker game plan researchers with lesser likelihood as her Partners who were the sole providers in the organization. Then again, they lived with me a two times as high likelihood in a logically homogeneous an organization. Figure 2.6 shows the probabilities for information researchers relying upon the interlacing plan of the doctorate, an experimentally homogeneous or sole to have a place with worker design after graduation. The reference is as in past area that word related field heterogeneous example.

Notwithstanding the word related construction, beginning and match qualities likewise the connection to one of the six example before the doctorate is considered (Figure 2.6), it very well may be seen that the Researchers who have the most elevated likelihood opportunities for a solitary worker model contrasted with a word related heterogeneity quality plan, were the ones that were at that point set up before the doctorate rehearsed this joining game plan. The distinctions among people this gathering are anyway outright: Researcher, who were the sole workers in the doctoral stage stayed after the movement with multiple times the likelihood with this joining as researchers.

Entanglement arrangements in the course of the pair

Figure 2.6: Probability of men and women for sole dual earner pattern that is homogeneous in terms of

servants and academics after the doctorate according to selected interdependence tern of the doctoral phase (reference: job field heterogeneous Pattern)

2.5 The interdependence of scientists in the family history

As discussed in the second section, family events can also lead to a "change of interdependence". To examine how couples after the birth of their first child, a different marriage arrangement to practice their activities, it is first necessary to understand the patterns in the two years before the birth of first bodily child short to represent around so a comparison with the later arrangements to allow.

The analysis of the interdependence of employment trajectories of scientific parents and their partners before the birth of their first child shows four pattern (not shown). About 40% of the scientists and the scientific women lived in an occupationally heterogeneous double-earner arrangement mind. Significant gender differences can be found in the distribution from scientifically homogeneous and Single earner arrangements: former were clearly more often at scientists (32% vs. 18% in the men), the latter among male scientists (33% vs. 13% for women). For 10% of scientists and 14% of scientists workers was the interweaving through interruptions the Knowledge-business activity, be it due to gainful employment the partner outside the science system or non-employed abilities of the scientist. Essentially, then, the interrelationships pattern before the parenting those in the PhD phase very similar

– among other things, because most scientists only after the doctorate became parents (cf. chapter 3 in this book; Hess/Rusconi/ Solga 2011).

Figure 2.7 shows that in addition to the scientifically homogeneous and ruffeldheterogeneen dual earner patterns (Pattern 1 and 2) and to the single earner arrangement (Pattern 3) in the six years after the birth

That means, that, how in the Section 2.4.3 set out, no Single earner pattern due to the non-employment the scientists after the promotion to find is. of the first child there was an additional interweaving arrangement that due to a relatively long break in the academic career characterized by being inactive (9%, pattern #4 in Figures 2.7). [24] In addition, all patterns for the period after child desbirth more often phases with one others combination the activities on. A comparison of entanglement patterns before and after birth first child makes it clear , *firstly* , that the spread of double earnings couple after the birth removed has; namely from 72% on 53% – and this self then, if next to the both scientifically homogeneous and -heterogeneous dual earners also the dual earner shares the ge mixed group. *Secondly,* male che and female scientists after parenthood clearly in their Arrangements: Four times as many male as female scientists were sole earner (40 vs. 7%). On the other hand, almost a fifth of Female scientists (17%), but only two scientists themselves not employed. However, just over half of the scientists nen as well as 40% of the scientists were also after the birth of the first child part of one double earner couple. The birth of a child resulted so not inevitably to longer career breaks the Women (neither for the partners nor for the scientists). the up legal preservation of dual earner arrangement lies - such as the analysis will show in chapter 3 of this book – in the negotiation processes in the Pair as well as external support.

A comparison of the entanglement patterns before and after the birth of the first ted child at the individual level also shows that half of the knowledge who, before the birth of their first child, may have had an intertwining arrangement, this also afterwards practiced (54% of the scientists and 58% of the scientists). However, while 15% of the women in this group continue their work for a longer period, this was not the case for any man. However almost a fifth of the scientists and only one woman ner.

22

One something higher stability the interweaving pattern had Knowledge-workers in before occupational field heterogeneous Partnerships: 66% the Men and 63% of women continued this entanglement pattern. But even in this group, almost a fifth of the men and none of the women became Sole earner, while 9% of women and only one man after childbirth of the child their employment interrupted.

---

24 There is also a mixed phase for the phase after the birth of the first child group (20%; pattern no. 5) in which there is no dominant but alternating entanglement arrangements and many (censored) cases, ie where the interview before the sixth Birthday of child took place.

Entanglement arrangements in the course of the pair

the first child Intertwining patterns, however, those male scientists who are already *before* the birth sole earner were (80% vs. 36% the Women). However A quarter of the scientists in this group interrupted their employment activity while the partner became employed (27%). The rest of After the birth of their first child, scientists switched to socially homogeneous and in a few cases to occupationally heterogeneous double earner arrangements (18% and 4% respectively).

In summary, this means: Although dual earner partnerships especially for female scientists after the birth of their first child represent the majority interweaving arrangement, has parenthood an incisive and gendered meaning for men and women and for the intertwining of employment histories in couple relationships gene. This family Event leads straight at scientists and their partners to greater changes than the professional event of Promotion. The main reason for this is the persistence of gender more typical role pattern, the also at academic educated men and

women are common. The following will examine which properties of the scientists and their partners to pursue a bad-typical single-earner or single-earner arrangements after the birth of first child explain can and in what way earlier interweaving arrangements affect later.

Multivariate analyzes show that scientists - even after consideration of occupational structure, origin and couple characteristics - with ten times more likely than their peers after birth of the first child are the sole breadwinners for a longer period of time. science scientists interrupted however her own employment with double such a high probability like their colleagues. 25

How also for the interweaving pattern in the professional history shown became, is no rapprochement between male and female scientists of the younger graduating cohort. On the contrary: in equal to a (scientifically homogeneous or - heterogeneous) double servant arrangement gave it at the graduates the younger cohort even a higher probability for gender-typical single or Single-earner pattern than graduates who graduated before 1990 had acquired. With regard to the disciplines, the knowledge no differences, while male technical and natural scientists more likely than social scientists in Single Earner Partnerships lived. in summary can for the *occupational structural* characteristics are recorded that gender-typical Entanglement patterns after the birth of children to a greater extent younger graduates and male scientists in such named male-dominated disciplines (technology and natural sciences ten) were practiced.

With regard to the *characteristics of origin* , it can be stated that as expected Single earner arrangements after the birth of the first child with higher (almost twice) probability among West German scientists than could be found with their East German colleagues. The differences between West and East German female scientists in terms of single earner pattern were however significant lower. No noteworthy differences are found, on the other hand, between scientists whose mothers during of their childhood overwhelmingly employed were, and those whose mothers were mostly housewives. This means that a traditional division of labor in the family of origin reduces the probability to be employed at all (cf. section 2.4.3), but if this Women employed are, then place she after the birth of first child

25 For reasons of space, the estimated (linear probability) models for the entanglement development pattern after the birth of the first child not shown. You are with the author on Inquiry available.

Entanglement arrangements in the course of the pair

her employment just as few to the disposition How her female colleagues from families of origin with a more egalitarian division of labor.

With regard to the *age constellation* in the partnership, a different influence on the interweaving patterns of the male and female Scientist. male scientist with untypical Age constellation (ie in which the partner or the scientist older was) practiced after the birth of first child with bigger Probability of a gender-typical sole breadwinner arrangement than her Colleagues with others age constellations. However distinguished women scientists who were older than their partners with regard to their Probability for single earner arrangements not from their peers with a typical age constellation or those of the same age. For the family phase after the birth of the first child cannot be confirmed, that the probability from dual earner arrangements at aged atypical couples is higher. All of these findings point to a significant Persistent gender role patterns after the birth of children there.

With regard to the importance of earlier interdependence patterns, the evidence found a clear stability of the entanglement pattern (Figure 2.8). The highest probability for a single earner arrangement

Figure 2.8: Probability in men and women for single and Single earner pattern after the birth of the first child after selected interweaving patterns before birth (reference renz: academically homogeneous and professionally heterogeneous Pattern)

sole earner after childbirth   single   earner   after
childbirth

2.6 Conclusion

In this chapter, the intertwining patterns of the employment histories in pairs of academics and their dynamics. Essentially exist- four entanglement patterns: two patterns in which both partners are active (occupational field heterogeneous and scientifically homogeneous double earnings nerarrangements), and two patterns where only one of the two partners is in paid employment (researcher or partner). However, the spread of this interweaving pattern is chen professional and family phases as well as between scientists and Female scientists "unequally" distributed.

Dual Earner Partnerships put for scientists the represent the majority of interdependence patterns in all professional and family phases, while among their male colleagues they are somewhat less frequent and according to birth of the first child were on par with the single breadwinner pattern. Also because of ours study population – scientific employees

– the (temporary) non-employment of scientists was relative rarely, but in two phases of life, especially in female scientists to to find: in the PhD phase and after the birth of first child

Entanglement arrangements in the course of the pair

des. The sole employment of the scientist, on the other hand, came in all phases, but was more common in male scientists in the PhD phase and before everything after the birth of first child to. In In all professional and family phases there were therefore gender-typical opportunities for certain interdependence patterns as well as for changes in interdependence tion after the doctorate or the birth of the first child.

It should be emphasized that this gender-typical

distribution of single, single and dual earner models is *not* an "outdated" Phenomenon that mainly scientists of the older graduating cohorts. Precisely the expectation of an mend similarity between scientists and scientists the younger graduating cohort could not confirmed become. Quite in the Opposite: Both for the doctoral phase and for the phase after birth of first child gave it at the graduates the younger Cohort even a higher probability for the sex-specific Practicing single-breadwinner patterns. The findings for the male scientists suggest that the conditions for double pelverinnerarrangements deteriorated have. risen Requirements to the scientists - such as a higher career relevance of third- fundraising, publications in English speaking magazines (see. Munch 2006) and stays abroad – tied together with one further Precariousness of the scientific middle faculty (cf. Gülker 2010). on the one hand the risk of a single-earner pattern (e.g. due to involuntary eng career breaks) increase, on the other hand but also the one single-earner pattern when attempting to cope with inactivity the partner the flexible use under constant proving of the knowledge schafters to allow.

In this regard, it should also be emphasized that Genetic dual earner arrangements are comparatively risky or unstable are. This is especially true in the partnerships of male scientists to determine. After the doctorate of the scientists with one before scientifically homogeneous dual earner pattern was one long-term non-employment with the partners of the scientists double so probably How at the partners the scientists. At latter found rather a Change of occupation as non-employment instead of. given ours study population, in the only under the Partners can be found people who have left science, is of that to go out that the here presented Results the exit of women in science even underestimate.

However, the findings also show a clear stability of the interdependencies development patterns across the professional and family phases. After the promo tion and after the birth of the first child (occupational heterogeneous or. scientifically homogeneous) dual earner pattern before everything at those to find couples who already have such intertwining patterns in the phases before. The "points" for the interweaving of employment histories in So partnerships were established early in the career. this applies but also for male scientists and their partners on their own earner pattern: They also had a high probability that they continue this pattern in later stages of life. On the other hand tend to adopt the single-earner pattern among scientists and their partners temporary arrangement 26

–

Finally is to emphasize that Dual Earner Partnerships are very common and among scientists also after the birth of the first child represent the majority pattern of interdependence. nevertheless it is a myth that academic couples are usually dual earners. Even among the female scientists – a positively selected group – shows long-term (!) interruptions. The phenomenon is even more underestimated when considering the arrangements of their male colleagues or of the partners of the colleagues considered. That means the promotion of ration of women in science needs a clear improvement the general conditions for dual earner couples, and this already in earlier career phases (promotional and postdoc phase), as well as for one Return to work in general and to science special.

---

26 Since women (and men) who do science due to their own non-employment ness but are not living in a partnership with a scientist, are not included in our

sample, the spread of the nerpatterns underestimated.

3. Career with a child in science – Egalitarian claim and traditional reality of family care arrangements successful Women and their partners

3.1   Career barrier child?

"Oh, Ms. Neubert, are you still in science? You have two now Children." (Professor, three children)

Science represents a professional field in which women with children in leadership positions are rare. Only every third to fifth professor sorin, but more than every second professor has one or more children (cf. Lind 2008; Metz-Göckel/Selent/Schuermann 2010). In connection withthe Ask after career opportunities from high qualified Women becomes the Having children is still the "number one obstacle to careers" discussed. In this chapter we want to specifically pursue the question of which influence of children on the career development of women in science have.

Universities and colleges are a field of activity in which those success for those who base their entire life on science and research (cf. Engler 2001). A scientific career re is in the Rule with one high personal Mission as well as long working hours and lengthy qualification phases (cf. Beaufaÿs 2005). The classic characteristics of professional activity as Scientists correspond to those in many respects other academic professions with independent areas of responsibility and management tasks: High and flexible time availability skill requirements (at the day, weekly and annual working time) as well as high demands on geographic mobility. Added to that a career in science over a long period of time no secure employment perspective offers. Nevertheless is one slight trend turn of the well-known image of childless female scientists perceptible: The Portion PhD Women with children and PhD Women without

Children in leadership positions is the same in and outside of academia high (cf. Schubert/Engelage 2010), and female professors with children a family earlier in life than their older colleagues (cf. Zimmer/Krimmer/Stallmann 2007). A closer look at women who are pursuing a scientific career with a child shows that they often do not have the desired number of children because they are born at birth several Children negative consequences for her science careers anticipate. Also treasure scientists her professional Future rather pessimistic one, although they are central to their profession grant and in this one attractive career perspective see (see. Lind 2008). In general, highly qualified women with families must half of science with disadvantages in terms of their professional mobility and accept the associated loss of income (cf. Schu- bert/Engelage 2010).

The career disadvantages of women in science described here however, do not go back to starting a family per se, but to the with the childcare related professional Restrictions, How several months of career breaks, reduced working hours, lower Attendance times or the restriction of spatial mobility, such as new ones research results show (see. Metz-Göckel/Selent/Schuermann 2010). Especially in the first year of life, but also later, scientific Most women learn the main responsibility for caring for their children (cf. Hess/Rusconi/Solga 2011a). Their male counterparts have more often Partners, the Not or only limited employment are, so that more often "the back is kept free" for their careers (cf. Hess/ Rusconi 2010). Female scientists only share information in rare cases your partners the care duties already in the first age of child (almost) equally. An exclusive child care through the partner often comes neither for the women nor the men itself into consideration. [1] Female scientists are thus – like other (employed) ge) Women too – with specific societal expectations of courage confronted. The "calls to motherhood", ie the societal scientific expectation at Women in modern companies, next to the gainful employment to prove oneself as a mother (cf. Correll 2010), at odds with the strong and comprehensive focus on tion of professional careers (cf. Reichart/Chesley/Moen 2007).

So far, little is known about how female scientists without a career bend her careers with children continue can. The testimonial

---

1 analyses showed that included often stereotypes normative expectations at parenting in posted, and if the partners work as scientists, Science constructed by its partners as a profession with spatial-temporal flexibility which, in contrast to other employment relationships, is based on freely selectable working hours the Care from children allows (see. Hess/Rusconi 2010).

Career with a child in science

te many scientists with child(ren) show, that this everything other as a matter of course (cf. Biller-Andorno et al. 2005). how high qualified women also pursue their careers with children – sometimes in very under- different ways – shows the study by Walther and Schaeffer-Hegel (2007) for non-academic careers. Generally They find that highly qualified women tend to raise their children get later in life, with the choice of timing not follows a consistent pattern and there is no ideal point in time could be determined subjectively or objectively. However, the authors can identify some of the success factors that make professional careers with children possible chen. On the one hand, this is the behavior of women, which is reflected in the mulation clearer Goals, the open Enter for the own Interests and characterize the sometimes high resilience. On the other hand, they confirmauthors that the direct re-entry after the maternity leave or after an interruption of a maximum of six months and the possibility ability to the flexible Work cheaper is for the professional Success from Women as long-term career breaks or part-time jobs gen. However, only women can be continuously and fully employed who have the certainty that their children will be cared for (at a high level) is guaranteed. According to Walter and Scheffer-Hegel, this usually sets a Combination of public or company childcare with additional lich Private funded childcare in advance. Not last prove itself the support of the partner "of elementary importance for the successful reconciliation of children and career" (Walther/Schaeffer- Hegel 2007: 19). Partners who share childcare with their wives share, support the careers of their wives not only practically, but also non-material and represent a moral strengthening for the scientists dar.

To what extent do these results affect the careers of women scientists are transferrable has not yet been adequately researched. We only begin to know how the careers of women with families develop in science (cf. Chapters 2 and 5 in this book). What remains unclear is which partnership negotiation processes are behind the realized childcare rangements hide and to what extent they affect the careers of scientists influence gutters. Both are the subject of this article. We're going assume that for highly skilled employed women and men who live as a couple in the same household and have children, conventional al *family economic cost-benefit considerations* (cf. Becker 1991) only very limited to wear come. They have a specialization the partner is less (less) attractive due to gainful employment *or housework* the high educational investments of both partners or this specialization becomes e.g. B. also not applicable due to smaller income differences strives. Simultaneously own other economic explanations How the *resource negotiation model* (cf. Ott 2001) a certain explanatory power for the division of childcare, provided that social expectations genes and standards are included. This approach takes the relative bargaining power between the partners before the starting a family as starting point for deciding how childcare is to be between the two partners. Starting from this basis based the decision making on rational considerations the Partner. They also act in anticipation of future labor market opportunities and con- concrete job offers whose career interruption is less serious has a negative effect on returning to work (cf. Pfahl/Reuyß 2009). The expectations of superiors and colleagues definitely play a role here an important role. The fact that tends to be the highly skilled Women and not their partners take parental leave can then be explained with that that couples should be encouraged or sanctioned to start a family through the Employer for Women and Men differing assess. They then decide despite equally high investments in education for the woman to take parental leave. This decision-making on the one hand due to the frequently younger age of the woman (compared to straight to her partner) and her therefore not so advanced cardio on the other hand due to segregation processes on the labor market women are more likely to work in jobs with fewer opportunities for advancement offer (cf. Rusconi/Solga 2008).

With reference to doing gender approaches, gender inequality must units, which are generated and reproduced in the actions of couples, but also on cultural beliefs the participants, How e.g. B. changed ideals of romantic love (cf. Herma 2009). Thus, the increasingly career-oriented life course decisions ments of women with highly qualified and well-earning partners understandable (see. Gildemeister/Robert 2008). Out of this perspective becomes the increasing proportion of men who have to take care of their children gifts take over and limit their working hours understandable.

The central characteristics of an academic career, such as the high electiveness, a low level of predictability and a high level of professional insecurity attainment of the professorship, suggest that *risky biographical over- such as starting* a family at a later point in time in the life course or career progression can be postponed. By reaching a solid position and the consequent consolidation of the scientific If you are late, starting a family may be less risky for you further career progression. From a life course perspective, it appears for career opportunities for women in science are therefore more favorable if the transition to parenthood in the career history done later.

3.2 *Question and method*

Against the background of these considerations and the results of the In terms of research, this article addresses two research questions: First becomes examined, which strategies scientists with child(ren) for develop the pursuit of their careers and what mentoring arrangements ments (with their partners) can be found when starting a family. At- Finally, it is examined what influence the solutions of the childcare ung on the career opportunities of female scientists. As part of this The focus of this article is on the differences between knowledge women with and without a career. With this approach we can Female scientists at the career levels below the professorship in our re include analyzes and findings that previously only . for female professors templates, complement. Conditions of success for the realization of family and scientific careers for women can thus be more appropriately show.

a *family* means the *birth of the first child* the. However, we also include non-biological children who are born in the lived in the same household. Starting a family is therefore an important Ges biographical event, because with the birth of the first child for the parents to the already existing professional and private commitments, new add time-consuming tasks. In contrast to this, we summarize the Birth(s) of all further children as a family extension, which we however only secondary take into account can. Because scientists and her Partners agree on the strategies and organization of the children's care differentiate, develop differing beneficial (or. disadvantageous) realization conditions for their careers after family founding.

In our analyses, the *concept of career is used in its formal meaning* tion used in science: We define that a person is a has a career if she completes her doctorate within six years and half of 16 years has completed her habilitation and an adequate occupies a professional position. In technical sciences, in which are realized less frequently, the assumption of management tasks be used as an equivalent criterion for a career (cf. Chapter 1 in this A book).

By *strategy* we mean the way in which individuals persecution from aim and Wish act. strategies own one normative dimension that can be reconstructed when partners express their cal and ideas about gainful employment and parenthood. We assume that strategies involve acting in different con- texts and thus also addressed to the scientists callous and social expectations be and process. Strategically act
means to act intentionally towards a goal, but not in narrow- to act in a calculative manner. This means that actors do not act with instruments mentally towards only one partial goal and can therefore develop their own strategies also "succumb". 2 To that extent own the strategies the couples with reference to of their professional Development as well as the partnership and Family a strengthen influence on the actual design of childcare.

When organizing childcare, we differentiate *between couples Care arrangements* from the *care services provided by third parties* . former means the division of responsibility for the care tasks among the partners and the implementation of these responsibilities in everyday life. grab it we go back to ideal typifications of the care arrangements: In one *traditional care arrangement,* the woman takes on the main responsibility for child care. In a *reverse traditional len care arrangement* it is the man. In an *egalitarian ungarment* split itself both partner the care duties equal kindly. The both first place so in demarcation to the egalitarian care arrangements represent hierarchical couple arrangements (cf. Rusconi/ Solga 2008). Third party support means the use of public Care facilities, childminders or the involvement of people from private networks into childcare. Both aspects, the paired internal care arrangement and external care work together, since the outsourcing of the care work by one or both parties better organized must become.

For our analysis, quantitative and qualitative methods are used binned. In the *first Step* becomes a short overview about it given, who of the scientists in academic partnerships a family establishes when this usually takes place and how many children are born. The study population for this and the other quantitative analyzes lyse consists out of the questioned scientists (target persons) with biological children or children who have lived in the same household from birth just lived. This and all following descriptive evaluations became weighted in terms of disciplines and career levels, so that the disci- plan always the same often are represented.

In the *second step* , we focus on the support strategies of the scientists and their partners. The basis for this evaluation 17 problem-centered interviews with female scientists form the next step with child(ren) and eleven problem-centered interviews with their partners. All here shown cases have for the interview time at least a personal

---

2 Borderline cases of action are also conceivable, which with Weber (1992 [1919]) as affective tive or traditional action can be described. In traditional action to no longer recognize an orientation towards the person's own goals; ie the social Obligation prevails.

Career with a child in science

ches child. [3] The interviews were conducted using the process-structured method ten topic comparison evaluated (see. joke 2000). The Testify the Respondents on individual subject areas and the design of the children's care arrangements became content analytical recorded (see. Mayring 2000), then condensed across all cases and contrasted with each other. In shortcut with the quantitative distribution the different Support arrangements for scientists and their partners are discussed let's explore the importance of these arrangements for professional careers by women. In the representations with a longitudinal section perspective, we refer focus mainly on three points in time or time periods: the first year of the child, his second and third year of life and his fourth to sixth year of life. The focus of our considerations is on matched by female scientists with and without career success *to the Inter- view time* . About it out take into account we also the male Scientists, since these serve as a benchmark for the context of high school important are.

In the *third* step, we use multivariate methods to check which flow the care arrangements for the first child on it own, ifespecially women at the various points in time after family founded according to objective specifications have careers in science or not. Following on from the longitudinal considerations in the descriptions analysis is carried out with regression models for panel data, to investigate the effects of the various influencing factors over time chen. [4]

---

[3] According to the career definition (see above), 13 of

these women have a company career. After starting a family, these women were either able to successfully continue their career (i.e. one year, three and six years after family foundation *and* at the time of the interview) or they had at least six years after the Starting a family or success in science at the time of the interview. Four more Women without a career are used as comparison cases; after having a family, they establishment and until for the interview time continuous no Career.

4 For this we use logistic random effects models. In it, the error term in divided into two components. A component is a time-constant error term between varies between the study units. It shows the average deviation of a person to the sample mean at. The second component is a error term, the both between the investigation units and between the observation time score varies. The is the real measurement error (see. Rabe-Hesketh/Skrondal   2005).   Time-constant influencing variables can also be taken into account with random effects models. genes that are relevant in our analyses. This includes e.g. B. the age constellation in the partnership or the employment status of the partner before starting a family as a nalization the negotiating position or the belonging to one subject group.

3.3 Scientific careers of women in partnership with child

"If I In the morning around eight here am, then am I one and a half Hours long the Only, and when I leave at five, there will be some commentary." (Juniorprofessorin, a child)

3.3.1 Who has Children, When and How many?

Table 3.1 provides an overview of some demographic indicators Family formation of the scientists, which we will refer to below for the Part relate. For the shares at Parents under scientists overall, our sample shows the same from previous research Familiar picture: Female scientists had fewer at the time of the interview children than their male counterparts. Female professors in particular (61%) have significantly fewer children than professors (85%), [5] while the differences between the sexes at the career levels below the Professorship less pronounced are.

scientists with Family have at the most common two Children (46%). However have scientists more often as her male Colleagues only one child. This difference is again with the professors particularly striking: While 41% of the mothers among female professors only one have a child, this only applies to 21% of the fathers among the professors. For women is the realization of family *and* professional success, especially re in a top position in science, i.e. more difficult than for men ner.

scientists are at the starting a family in the Average something younger as her male Colleagues (30.7 or. 32 Years). This Age difference roughly corresponds to that of the highly qualified in general mean (29.3 or 31 years; Federal Center for Health Education tion 2005: 7). The average age of academics in Akademikerpartnerships, on the other hand, is slightly higher than in general for women and men with college degrees. To study the influence of starting a family on the career opportunities, however, it is instructive cher, not that age, but that timing of the related to starting a family on

---

5 In other studies, female professors have even fewer children (cf. Zimmer/Krimmer/ Stallman 2007). This discrepancy could be related to that of us professors surveyed are relatively young on average and younger generations have children more often than older ones (cf. also Metz-Göckel/Selent/ Schuermann 2010). One further Explanation for the high proportion of female professors with child(ren) may be in the higher willingness to respond due to a higher interest at the Theme of project.
to look at the academic qualification and career progression. Included it can be said that half of the scientists have their first child born before graduation and the other half after graduation became. For a not inconsiderable part of the scientists, the Birth of the first child even before their first academic degree (11%). However, there are differences in the timing of starting a family Depending on the career level: For professors and postdocs (from three years after the doctorate), starting a family was more often in the period after the PhD (60%), while PhD students and postdocs (up to three years after the doctorate) was rather before the doctorate (82%). This sub The difference is due to the interaction of two aspects: first tens, careers in science come about through selection processes which the less advanced scientists still have to stand. Secondly, the aforementioned earlier timing of the parental shaft at to the younger scientists.
The transition to parenthood is not accidental for scientists, but mostly a highly planned affair. The clear

increase majority of scientists (72%) stated that the point in time for the birth of their first child was planned. However, the profession is at the tion this private Decision not in each case at first Job. Profession-Technical considerations only played a role here for 23% of the scientists an important or very important role.

Going beyond the usual differentiation according to career levels and looks at women with and without success in science At the time of the interview, it turns out that women with success are even less likely to have children have (44%) than the group of female professors. From these mothers with Career success nearly half have only one child (48%), and they found In the majority of cases, their families did not leave their families until after they had obtained their doctorate (55%). For the The family situation changes for women who are unsuccessful in science significantly different. A strikingly higher proportion of them have children (83%), and the mothers without career success have less common only a child (26%), ie they usually have two or more children. These scientists also started their families more often already before the doctorate (59%).

The differences in the family situation between women with and without Success in science cannot be explained by the fact that fewer successful scientists at career intentions missing and *that's why they* have children more often. Because it turns out that the pro-women scientists with child(ren) promoted significantly more often with determination want to stay in academia than childless (77 and 63% respectively). Those *with child(ren)* are much less likely to successfully pursue a career than those *without child(ren)* (51 and 82% respectively). In addition, it can be observed that female scientists with career success speed up starting a family rär or completely defer. They limit the number of children they have or postpone it starting their family. Because for the female scientists with a doctorate shows that the previously childless but successful among them in the plural theirs desire to have children still have not realized (80%), but only a mall proportion itself wants no children (20%).

3.3.2 *(No more correct Time?*

The subjective interpretations of the scientists also show that the scientific career is perceived as a professional path who are prevented by family-related interruptions or reduced working hours are. All interviewed female scientists with child(ren) report of Concerns about the "right time" to start a family. The coined consciousness for negative Follow in the Profession and the Fear before one

"Career setbacks" after starting a family prompt many women to self the Responsibility for the Succeed of their careers to attribute. The claim of women to be responsible for their own careers act leads to the scientists trying to give birth to plan their children precisely and often to a later, professionally more patibler time postpone. A fewer planning Act in the con text the family planning becomes from the respondents as "irresponsible"perceived.

The central motivation for the reprieve the starting a family isthe desire to first (at least) finish the doctorate, which is the central ler career step the scientific career perceived becomes (see Section 3.1). [6] The prospect of a reasonably secure job lich Perspective, the in the Science first to one comparatively reached at a late point in time is considered a further motive for scientificadvised to wait before starting a family. In addition to your own professional Getting ahead and financial security is also important for many Women important in the run-up to starting a family, with their partners being able to live *and* work in the same place. Is living together on the same not possible in one place without making (major) professional compromises, there is a majority of either a postponement of the desire to have children and/or a renunciation of children. It becomes very clear that the argument about the "right time" for the birth, a high emotional burden for the scientists (more than for their partners ner). They try, so to speak, to close the gap between different acting institutional logics of professional career and family to bridge. The absurdity of this rational planning family drawn events reflects itself not only in the Fear before professional disadvantages, but also in the fear for prevented parenthood contrary.

Against the background of the quantitative and qualitative findings that together on the enormous difficulties indicate with those Knowledge- workers around around the starting a family confronted are, judge we in the following three sections the View on the scientists and their partners: What are the strategies the scientists are trying to use? and their partners the professional and family requirements according to the to do justice to starting a family?

3.3.3 If not she, then he? care strategies from Women

"He was never asked, 'Man, how are you? And how does she deal with that? Even still scientist and now Mother. I became once in the Week asked: How does he deal with that? Man, can he stand it at all? Does he already have withdrawal apparitions?" (Scientific employee, one child)
The Scope, with to the the scientists and her partner in the are involved in caring for the children in the first year of life, leaves three different strategies of female scientists to reconcile children and recognize career.

---

6   as alternative becomes from some Women also called, Children possible early, i.e. H. before Diploma of study to get.
     The *first group* includes female scientists who do not have an egalitarian sharing of their partners in the care of the children in the first year of life expect and do not demand them at all or only to a very limited extent. The strategy this Women marks itself much more through this, that she the persecution of their professional Goals to to back up attempt, in which she the caring for their child themselves – and without the support of their partners – take over. mostly grasp she included on the Support from third party
ie either childcare facilities, childminders and/or turned, return. The sole takeover the primary responsibility the Child care is justified by biological arguments, like that Breastfeeding as a mandatory reason for the woman to be present, or with the social economic conditions and values, which are particularly important for women of older cohorts cannot be questioned in their normativity (could ten). That is take

itself the scientists across from your partners in the professional field as equals, for family life the difference is However, the difference between women and men is constitutive. Even with knowledge workers this Group, the younger cohorts belong, is applicable the main responsible takeover the childcare as one self-steadfastness. Nonetheless differentiate itself the interpretations the Women the older and younger cohorts: The women of the older cohorts *could* (in retrospect) due to the social framework no different than taking over the main responsibility for looking after the children men, and in this way tried to avoid conflicts with their partners who did not feel it was their duty to look after their children in. The women of the younger cohorts, on the other hand, would not *have it* any other way. She state that it is their explicit wish, the common children mainly self to care for. Particularly in the first age of child acceptthey limited their partners' involvement in childcare Wise and reject offers from their partners to take part in childcare participate, for the part off.

The support strategy of the scientists of this first hand group consists of, within the traditional gender division of labour in the childcare after solutions to look for which pursuing their professional careers after starting a family allow. Using sophisticated care strategies and the support third parties, these female scientists secure their professional advancement men. Only when the normative ideas (of caring for the child by one's own parents, ie in particular the mothers) application in the Finding ways to organize everyday family life and at the same time your own professional ones Ambitions are reduced, are the careers of women scientists for the Part endangered. [7] Is striking, that the diverse legitimacy for the

7 This was shown by a comparison with women who did not (any longer) have a career after starting a family. have. For this scientists without professional Success showed itself, that the realistic
main supply the Children through the Women in particular at Knowledge-female scientists can be found in the technical and natural sciences (to career orientations see chapter 4 in this A book).

For the scientists in the *second* and *third groups,* the Supporting the partner discursively plays an important role in coping family and professional requirements after starting a family. The The question of childcare takes up a lot of space with these women communication with the partner. It's about looking after the family not to allow any "asymmetry" to develop in the partnership. Sharing the mentoring work is important for these scientists important aspect of the desired symmetry in the couple relationship. Normative gender equality is not only discussed here in working life, rather also in the family life went out. One egalitarian family division of labour becomes in Relation on the professional Development the Women as well as in the importance for the partnership and the father-child relationship considered important. The central point is that childcare is independent of all knowledge female workers is generally perceived as a professional hurdle and the gainful employment at many as "the fewer exhausting" is applicable. The expectation of equality this scientists directs consequently up the personal relationship *of both* partners to theirs child and each other.
However, precise analysis shows that the strategy is about participation of their partners in childcare their status as professional and family To secure the same after starting a family, for the scientific the second group in the first year of the child's life only to a very limited extent rises. In fact, women take on more caring

responsibilities than theirs Partner. Partner support for childcare can be described as more symbolic Contribution characterize, How e.g. B. the takeover from two"Father's months" or stepping in in "emergencies". Despite the unequal distribution of parental leave or reduced working hours, equal health expectations at the partner discursive maintain. The Knowledge- scientists develop a variety of legitimation strategies in order to gene Mission of their partner and the discrepancy between the formulated expectations and the gender typical division of labour in the family area to justify. In addition to biological arguments, such as those are formulated for the women in the first group, the women argue this group additionally with the different logic of the professional field of their Partner. The scientific Profession is applicable because of his spatial temporal supposedly more flexible job opportunities as the one, the could be better reconciled with the care of children, so that these gabe in partnerships in which the partner outside of science is busy the scientists falls to (see. Hess/Rusconi 2010).

ization traditional care arrangements at simultaneous reduction professional ambitions for the professional Development from Disadvantage is.

Unlike the women in the first group, who do not try to to involve them in the care of their children, they report Scientists of the second group of conflictual negotiations with their partners. The desire for equality with the partner is not only in the professional Area, rather also in the Family leads in addition, that these women only organize support from third parties at a late stage – often after which they have "painfully" realized that their partners do not have the desired take over the largest part of the care tasks. Although this means that professional careers are not directly endangered, but the negotiations with these scientists cost the partner a lot of time and energy. For two- The first group consists primarily of female natural and social scientists, with it is striking that many of their partners are outside of science are active.

Finally can the scientists the *third group* her Expectations of equality in work *and* family with their partners actually implement. Either both go on parental leave equally, or the partners wear the same after a very short parental leave of the female scientists Responsibility for the Childcare. Is the latter the Case, ie go the partners themselves are not on parental leave, they reduce their working hours for them child care and/or make arrangements with the employer that it allow, that she above particular periods for the childcare able to work flexible hours. Although it (from the perspective of the Employers) can certainly make a difference that women tend to parental leave and men are more likely to take advantage of flexible working time models men, the distribution of caregiving tasks is shared by the couples table perceived. The perceived equality with the partner is through supports an open culture of discussion, in which the perfect balance between gainful employment and family responsibilities *for both* partners as well as the societal expectations with which *both* partners relate of parenthood are addressed. For the third group of female scientists – in contrast to the second group – the Strategy about involving their partners in their childcare Position as professional and family equal even after starting a family to back up, on. It is striking that this group *only* includes social scientists women or science-critical, feminist "politicized" natural science members. 8th In addition, the partners of the scientific are also mostly working as scientists or in science-related positions professions.

A *fourth group* with a *reverse traditional model* exists not in the true sense. Although a scientist from the Sam- please the partner the Care of common child already in the first

---

8 An exception is a technology scientist whose partner comes from a large family Family comes and the cooperation ,at the Family' used is.

age of the child mainly responsible. He himself pursues no career intentions and had to not on a Career waive.

It became clearly, that care strategies not from the Knowledge- women alone, but together with the partners are "made" the. In the next step, expectations and action strategies of the female scientists therefore complemented those of the partners.

3.3.4 *If not he, then she? care strategies from men*

"Who's picking up our son? First ignition is my wife, second stage are the grand parents, and if nothing works, then I'll do it." (Employee in a company man, a child)
Complementary to those female scientists the at the Children- care do not "count" on their partners and these tasks early on Outsource to third parties, some partners shows that the low participation of men in childcare tasks through their own traditional positions of the sexual division of labor (with). With a clear focus on one's own profession and with the consideration of childcare as "women's thing" support the *at childcare disinterested partner,* the unequal distribution of parental care at.

Most of the partners of the scientists we interviewed However, she prefers to get involved in childcare alongside her career and to bring into family life. [9] But there are some of these *Partners interested in childcare* who express their interest in family Matters not in practical support for various reasons implement and do not participate equally in childcare. Especially in the first year of the child's life, none of these men leave on parental leave or reduced working hours. This is justified either with the same biologisms as with the female scientists, the spatial temporal supposedly more flexible job opportunities of their partners or with it, that to size caveats of own employer expected become. Some partners participate in childcare and the their assigned times and tasks. However, all organi- satorical concerns at the Women, the on her Men as resource for

"emergencies" To fall back on.

Other *men interested in mentoring* feel through their professional position in her role as a father and would like to more care duties take over. Some fathers, the from your partner

---

9 This hangs also with it together, that for the qualitative sample overwhelmingly partner with
"atypical", i.e. H. from the model the gendered division of labour differ- en care arrangements selected became (see. Chapter 1 in this A book).

women who have been relegated to the position of breadwinner feel through the task, in case of doubt for the entire family income alone having to pay is a burden. They fear that there will not be sufficient economic to be able to guarantee mixed security for the whole family, and wish their partners would hand over part of the childcare and participate more in working life. This desire becomes particular then intensified when they work on fixed-term contracts and the pressure possible fast into a firm position switch, to the burden becomes.

Finally, there are *partners interested in childcare* who initially child take parental leave or reduce their working hours re. These regard the tasks related to raising children as self- understandability and have egalitarian ideas of a couple relationship hungry For these men, caring for their children represents a value in itself that they, as fathers, want to help shape. Adjust yours accordingly working hours thereafter out of and limit her professional availabilities a. This is made possible by the orientation towards a double-income household. The men interviewed rely on the women to have a contribute a more or less equal part of the income and the The existence of the family is thus doubly secured. The equal Gainful employment for women becomes a guarantee of prosperity and reduces risks in their own professional biography. These men therefore also have more sity and time because they suffer disadvantages from their own career breaks fewer have to fear.

Other partners see the phases of childcare as a "time out". own, unsatisfactory professional activities. maternity leave for older children (not the first year of life) are also used to to do business work, not to register as unemployed or to extend existing contracts and thus to plan career paths. Only in In a small number of cases, the partners' desire for equal participation commitment to childcare in the first year of the child's life primary responsibility for this. One primary responsibility the partner for the Childcare in the sense of a reverse traditional care arrangement gements is particularly encouraged if the partner himself does not is gainfully employed or has his/her position at the family's main place of residence and the partner to her place of work commutes.

It becomes very clear that starting a family is an organizational one and emotional attunement performance of couples based on different che way succeeds and is mastered. The following are the descriptive Findings of the different care expectancies, strategies and arrangements thoroughly discussed. Particular attention is paid to the frame set conditions within which the couples opt for certain arrangements gestures decide.

3.3.5 *Egalitarian Claim and handed down reality*

The evaluation of the quantitative data also confirms that under the asked always still the couples predominate, at those the Care the common children in the first year of life mainly responsible for the women in lies. Figure shows the division of care work within the couple 3.1, How itself the scientists with and without career success for the time of the interview on the various partnership-based care rangements over the periods of a) first year of life, b) second and third as well as c) Distribute the child's fourth to sixth year of life. [10]

Figure 3.1: Percentages of care arrangements within couples by age year of birth of first child and career at interview timepoint (in %, only female scientists)

Source: record "Together Career make"; own calculations; weighted Declarations

Overall, the care arrangements based on partnership gestures at both groups from scientists right similar. Until by the age of three of the first child, the so-called traditional nelle arrangement. From the qualitative interviews with women with success in the Science knowledge we, that some this couples "unwanted" traditional

---

10 This periods became chosen, there she through different institutions structured (such as through childcare facilities and their availability) and through legal maternity leave.

follow normal patterns. On the one hand, this affects

women who Not (fully) realizing the right to an egalitarian division of care because the partners prioritize other goals. On the other hand, it concerns also some partners who - unless their wives want more participation - schen – their desire for greater involvement in the care of the Children not implement can. The reasons for discrepancies between desire and reality in coping with child and career therewith on the expectations and action strategies as well as the Knowledge- employees and their partners. The traditional gender The division of labor in care work is therefore not the sole result of "un- willing", men who focus solely on working life, but for Part also the scientists themselves.

couples, the Responsibility for the Care the common Children take over together from the beginning, i.e. also in the first year of the child's life child, are also under high qualified and professionally ambitious Rather atypical for couples. Only in pre-school age are egalitarian childcare arrangements gements most common. This is certainly related to that for children of this age public care facilities are significantly better developed than for children under the age of three. [11] In the young ger cohorts of female scientists seem to be aware of the contours of increase of this novel partnership arrangement. These couples are characterized by a good knowledge of the discourses surrounding the Gender equality and know about the pitfalls of Science careers for women. They develop practices that deviate from the traditional pattern of gender division of labour. decision dend is in favor of the partner taking on the childcare fulfill their task as a father and thus make it easier for their partners to continue to work. Fathers realize this by themselves in Take parental leave or reliably reduce working hours. it is crucial that this partner their children not only in exceptional situations care for, such as when appointments are postponed or business trips, but regularly in the Care integrated are and for this in which case professional swabsaccept.

The reverse traditional care arrangement, in which predominantly the man who takes responsibility for childcare is under Female scientists not very common. However, there is a difference between scientists with and such without career success in this,

---

11 For the relative division of childcare between the partners, this means that the egalitarian arrangements may stem from the fact that there are womenen succeed in substituting part of the childcare with external care and to reduce the care work they have done themselves. The absolute contribution of men to care work does not necessarily have to change, it just shifts lich the relation in favor of one egalitarian care arrangements in the Partnership.

that the more successful women are somewhat more likely to be liary obligations are relieved and they can be used for their scientific chen activity the "back is kept free".

The findings to the partnership care arrangements the Female scientists are now subject to the situation of their male colleagues face gene. For men in science with children it is traditional care arrangement in the partnership for the most part of them, and not just in the first year after starting a family education, but up to the pre-school age of the child (without figure: 81% in first year of life, 69% from the second year of life). scientists have also much more common consistently traditional arrangements at the childcare than their female peers (55 and 36% respectively). So here they are wearing partners of the scientists the overriding concern for the common same kid, what for the careers of has a relieving effect on men.

The Evaluation the qualitative interviews has shown, that straight Female scientists with traditional support arrangements solutions outside of their partnership and are dependent on it in order to not to lose touch: with the help of external child care through institutions, au pairs or relatives they manage to child and reconcile careers. These women are extremely flexible; she organize their work around childcare hours and work also during her maternity leave at articles or qualification work.

The importance of third-party mentoring in organizing children The care is also reflected in the quantitative analyses. Figure 3.2 illustrates the distribution of female scientists with and without success at the time of the interview on the various possible combinations possibilities of external care for the first child. Analogous to the In the case of internal couple care, the description refers to the same periods. 12

In the partnerships of female scientists with career success the already in the *first age* of child majority Third in the Care included: Most often they exclusively access private ones persons return (35%). A not irrelevant Portion the couples might however, either by public care institutions or by theirs Combination with private use (together 41%). 15% of Women who were successful in science used childcare facilities in the child's first year of life all day or more than seven hours daily.

---

12 The category "care facility only" includes both public institutions and also market-mediated solutions such as e.g. B. Childminders together. The category "only pri-father Persons" includes the regular inclusion another family member and from Friends, but also babysitters

or other Persons.

With increasing Old of child relate (until on exceptional cases) nearly all of these couples using outside options for caring for their first child a. For *mothers with career success,* third-party care is a combination of care facilities and private individuals is of particular importance tion. Already from the second and third year of the child use 51%, at the pre-school age of the child, 64% of female scientists have one Combination. Overall, the proportion of female scientists who her child Full-time or longer by day-care centers, by 47% im Small child- to 60% im preschool age

Women unsuccessful in science relate to a very similar Instruct third parties to take care of their child, such as women with child(ren) and career success. This similarity lies in particular in the first age before. differences show itself but away to the second and third age of the child. From then on, women without career success reach out much more frequently finally to care facilities and more rarely to the combination solution than the mothers with career success. In addition, mothers leave without Career success their first child more often full-time or longer from childcare facilities than the mothers with career success (not shown: 22% and 15% in the first year of life, 59% and 47% in the second and third year Age, 71% or. 60% in the preschool age). This means however, that these scientists are more concerned about the opening hours of the than their colleagues, who also have to focus on private ones (can) fall back on caregivers. That could be a clue be that the female scientists without career success in their possibilities The ability to use external care solutions flexibly, above all, is restricted are - be it due to a lack of offers, financial or social resources.

Ultimately, the necessity of the combination solution is also connection with the care patterns within the partnerships. Because female scientists with children only stand up in the rarest of cases partner to the Page, the the main childcare takes over. There but the provision of care in the public sector together with the the burden of caregiving within the partnership is insufficient, the scientists have to do this through private solutions of the external supplement care.

In contrast to the female scientists, in partnerships with scientists in the different age ranges of the children more often "forgo" the care of third parties (no figure: 47% in the first year of life, 24% in the second and third year of life, 3% in school age). It is also noticeable that among the scientists the exclusive common use of facilities increases more than the combination of facilities and private persons to the childcare (57% or. 39% pre-school age) – similar to women without career success. All- However, their first child visits much less often all day or longer than they ben hours a day a care facility (not shown: 8% in first year of life, 31% in the second and third year of life, 43% in school age). That is, with the scientists it is not themselves, but primarily their partners, who take care of the children take.

In order to understand why traditional patterns of division of labor have also changed among highly qualified women and men after starting a family reproduce, it is important to also look at the context in which which the couples act. In the introduction, reference was made to the science system , which largely underscores the model of the male sole breadwinner. puts. Couples who organize childcare in an egalitarian way resist to a certain extent the prevailing expectations. For women, this means a large part of the care tasks against social reservations ben to their partners (or third parties), and for men to find out about the caveats of their (male) Colleagues and

superiors to override
ie to take more than the "symbolic" two months of paternity leave or to work part-time. In return, the action of couples who cannot implement their expectations of equality, as an adjustment performance at the prevailing structures seen become. How we
shown have, can as well as the women as well as the men ones be the ones who force this adaptation; depending on which job lien and social environment they move.

The interviews showed that the work contexts in which the scientists and their partners work are crucial to to develop strategies that go beyond a traditional gendered division of labour go out. In the interpretations of the scientists are repeated named some key factors that – regardless of the partnership Arrangement – contribute to the success of your professional development with a child gen. In addition to the possibility of individually designed working hours and flexible attendance times, the rhythm and length of commuting sen between place of residence and place of work, these are also the attitudes of the employers, Female colleagues and mentors. work contexts, in in which gender roles are reflected, in which colleagues with are busy with the same topic and act as role models stronger equal care solutions.

In the qualitative analysis it was also noticeable that egalitarian care ing arrangements are typically found among female social scientists were, while in the other disciplines, especially in the technical science, are rather atypical. This is also reflected in the quantitative Data. A total of 36% of the female scientists practiced common a traditional arrangement in their partnerships (no pictures tion): In the technical and natural sciences, women with card Criminal success is more often the primary responsibility for their child than those without career success (46% and 24%

respectively), but the former use it slightly more external care than the latter (82% and 71% respectively). In the social science, on the other hand, the relationship is reversed. There the woman-successfully consistently traditional arrangements than their colleagues women without success (29% and 45% respectively). A possible explanation why Female technologists are less likely to have egalitarian expectations of their partners formulate, could go back to the dominance of male work colleagues be led. Since they often have partners who have their "back for professional Keep requirements free", it can be assumed that that Theme childcare at the Workplace in total fewer present is. Women in technical professions also have children with them without their own Reserved across from your competencies to battle (see. Konekamp 2007). The sole assumption of childcare tasks could on to aim additional recognition for this to win, the them in the male dominated professional field withheld becomes. But also for Men these work contexts represent obstacles for their desires after parental leave or reduced working hours. Because the majority of their peers and superiors is employed full-time, it is not the case for men either light, support requests across from your employers and Female colleagues enforce. For the scientists and their partners, it represents a Significant relief when their superiors are dealing with Flexibility requests regarding working hours and place of work fully show and plan appointments and events on the Parents' obligations are respected. In order to be able to did not allow them to connect to work and professional networks lose, from the perspective of many scientists it is also important right, while the parental leave the contact to your superiors hold to and in some cases continue to work during parental leave. In the Interpretations of the scientists repeatedly showed how this Motivation to go to work as soon as possible after the birth of the child return is increased.

Despite the rather sobering findings on the gender division of labor There are signs of change among the scientists and their partners that traditional patterns are slowly breaking down. In the qualitative analysis was shown with regard to the professional careers of female scientists that different strategies can lead to the "same" goal. So Some female scientists secure their professional success through the outsourcing the childcare at Third, other above the parity Division of tasks with the partner. Nevertheless, it became clear that certain Strategies can also lead to a professional trap. The sole taking on the responsibility for supervision challenges the female scientists in addition a lot of organizational work from gainful employment. Vice versa cost the disputes with partners about the support tasks, the scientists additionally to the gainful employment also much Energy. In In both cases, these private coordination services do not correspond to the ideal-typical requirements for the realization one scientific chen career that has a high focus on and a dedication to require a job (cf. Engler 2001).

3.3.6 *career opportunities and employment histories*

In the following, we examine the influence of the various partnership technical support arrangements on the career success of female scientists to. We look at all female scientists with children and draw the male scientist with children as comparison group.

Figure 3.3 shows the proportions of women and men who which points in time before and after starting a family Success in science had or not. Here it can be seen that women a year ago are almost as successful in starting a family as men (time point: -12). Among women has a share of 69%, among men 72% one Career. First after the starting a family result itself clear gender typical differences in the chances of success.

Female scientists often experience career disadvantages after family Foundation: A year after the birth of the first child, the share begins female scientists with a successful career dropped to 61%. He recovers in the following observation times, stagnates however, around 63%. The proportion of successful knowledge six years after starting a family, women do not have the starting level as it was a year before starting a family. Accordingly the proportion of women without success in science increases over time. Overall, only 41% of the female scientists succeed in founding consistently at all observed points in time according to objective ven standards one Career to realize. For the Men, on the other hand, go the starting a family with stable career histories along. A Year after the birth of the first child, the proportion of scientists with success initially to 78% and then remains relative stable. In contrast to the female scientists, 64% of the men have a career throughout. experiences of discrimination and subsequent mothers are affected by relegations or exits from science (cooling-out). therefore in the rule more often than fathers (from Stebut 2003).

In the following dedicate we us the Compare within the group the scientists and place those with and without career success at the time of the interview. Figure 3.4 shows for both groups a history graph. It accumulates the relative proportions of the various Activity types of female scientists on a monthly basis 100% and shows, beginning with the twelfth month *before* the birth of the first child until for the 72 Month *after*, the relative proportions the respective activities.

Figure 3.4: Monthly activity status over a year before and six years after starting a family, accumulated percentage te: (a) scientists with career success to inter view point in time, (b) female scientists without career success for the interview time A first View on the graphics shows, that the gradients from Women with andwithout Success in the Science for the interview time one certain similar show viability. They are both quite "colorful", ie the gradients include a number of very different activities. Employed activities for all female scientists with children. Another similar-ability is shown by the fact that the courses of women with and without career hardly differ from each other for the time *before starting a family:* Approx. 61% of the female scientists work full-time, approx. 20% part-time employment, and about 10% have a scholarship. Those shares stay stable right up to starting a family.

In the first year after the birth of the first child, a ne large group of women mainly in parental leave and the proportion of employed women is declining. But especially at this time then there are differences in the career paths of female scientists determined. Almost half of the female scientists who later are successful generally take parental leave in the observed period Entitlement (47%). Their first parenting periods last on average 13 months on. Their use of parental leave is shaped over time as follows: The highest Portion at successful scientists 39% take parental leave in the fourth month after the birth, exactly one year after the birth are it 21%. This Share continues first return, but then rises again to 14% in the third year after starting a family at. Female scientists with other younger children are increasingly going here (again) on maternity leave. That is six years after starting a family only still 4% of women with success in the science in maternity leave

The employment histories of female scientists who at the time of the interview point *none* career success register can, see however something different out of. So take she generally something more often parenting periods in Entitlement (54%). Their first periods of upbringing also last with an average lich 18 months clearly longer as the of their female colleagues with career success.

The highest proportion of these female scientists on parental leave is 49% found as early as the first month after birth, a year after birth it is still 27%. This proportion then follows up to the third year only hesitantly to 14% before starting a family and is stabilizing this level up to child's sixth year of life.

The scientists without career success are after the family accordingly fewer employed. A year after the family 60% of them go into paid employment. In the third and sixth Year after the starting a family are that is 70% this Knowledge- female employees are employed, but the proportion has meanwhile been falling again due to the birth of more children. At the end of the considered time room reach the women who do not have success in science during the interview had not the baseline level of employment from the year before the starting a family. About it out moves itself at them in the Course the time *after* starting a family, the ratio of part-time to full-time activities in favor of part-time jobs.

Women who are successful in science, on the other hand, tend to figer into gainful employment after starting a family or return home afterwards return to the labor market faster than their colleagues without long-term towards career success. A year after starting a family, 65% of them are later successful female scientists employed, also in full-time positions, and this proportion increases steadily to 85% by the sixth year. With it is the starting level from a year before starting a family easily surpassed. Similar to her colleagues without career success the ratio of part-time to full-time jobs is shifting for them slightly in favor of part-time jobs six years after starting a familyten.

In summary, it can be stated that the proportion of full-time working mothers *without* success in science at no time after founding a family has reached a level comparable to that of academic scientists *with* success at the time of the interview. It is also noticeable that not only do parenting periods play a greater role for them, but that temporarily more affected by unemployment after starting a family and are more often financed by grants than female scientists with *success* . Compared to the career paths of the scientific with children are the courses of scientists with children in characterized primarily by full-time employment (on average 80%); the Starting a family as an event is in no way represented by change or Break-ins recognizable (not shown).

3.3.7 *Care arrangements influence science careers*

The results so far focus on the separate influences of individuals factors. In this section, these influencing variables are presented in regression models are brought together in order to take into account all factors appreciate the influence of the care solutions on the chance of be successful among women in science. We want about the previous comparisons, in which career success at the time point of the interview was the decisive criterion. In the models can now be checked whether women at the *various* points in time after the starting a family after objective Requirements Success in the Science had or not. All scientists were included in the calculations children included. In Table 3.2, the estimators are given as odds ratios and their confidence intervals [13] listed.

---

13 odds ratios give the odds ratio for the Enter one maternity between one Reference- and one comparison group at. A odds ratio from 1 means, that it nonecThere is difference in chance between the two groups. The comparison group has a higher chance than the reference group with an odds ratio of >1 and a low re chance with an odds ratio of <1. The confidence interval shows whether the estimated odds ratio lies within the given range with a probability of 0.95. The Estimate is uncertain if the value 1 is within the confidence interval and the greater better the confidence interval is.

Model 1 contains all theoretically relevant factors, model 2 contains them additional interaction effects of the care arrangement with the time run For the analysis of the organization of childcare, two restrictions in the Comparison to the descriptions in the preceded Section met become. Firstly, for external support only looked at whether it was used or not, and on the other hand ten the egalitarian and the opposite traditional couple arrangements at the childcare due to low case numbers combined become.

In the first Model shows itself, that for scientists after the starting a family there is a lower chance of having career success, if they are the ones in their partnership who are the main bear responsibility for child care (traditional arrangement). The use from external care options in turn improved the Outlook of mothers on career success in of science significant.

A detailed look at the impact of care solutions for the different points in time after starting a family in model 2 examines the entanglement relationship between the pair arrangement and the observation times and shows, that both effects itself clearly strengthen and at statistical significance gain weight. Because of the additional interaction terms are given by the estimator for the care arrangement ment in model 2 only indicates its influence in the first year of life of the child. Therefore is the chance on career success with female scientists with a traditional arrangement already in the first year of the child's life significantly less than their colleagues with non-traditional arrangements ment. The overall effect of the traditional care arrangement in Mo- dell 2 is additionally calculated from the effects of the interaction terms, ie overall, female scientists have a low chance of to have professional success after starting a family if they do the main lich jurisdiction for the Care hers child take over. To use scientists – independent from the pair internal care arrangement ment - the support of third parties in the care of their children, so is also the chance on career success greater. In Model 2 becomes aside from that It can be seen that the chances of career success increase in the sixth year of the Compared to the first year after starting a family, especially in the improve significantly, whose care arrangements within the couple ment does not follow the traditional model. This shows very impressive full, How important the partnership care arrangement after the Starting a family for the further career prospects of scientists actually run is.

Few surprised is the Result, that itself the opportunities on Success in science for mothers better design if they are already before successful in starting a family. For the hypothesis from the life-course perspective, that the career opportunities higher are, if the crossing to the parenting later in the career history he follows, leaves itself one careful Show confirmation: Female scientists who only had their first child after the promotion get, have a better chance of career success after starting a family (model 2). However, this result is only based on 10% level significant.

For the hypotheses of resource negotiation model find we no such clear and reliable findings. The relative negotiation position can be determined via the employment status of the partner before starting a family capture. The effects for this influencing factor are not significant edge, but they point in a certain direction. female scientists, whose partner before the starting a family one part-time employment pursued or financed by a scholarship tended to have better qualifications view career success than their full-time counterparts partners. The category "not gainfully employed" includes a number of different activities together, including training and internships ka. These are activities that actually mean full-time commitment and therefore tend to have a negative impact on the career prospects of scientists women scientists in connection with starting a family to.

the same models for the fathers under the scientists show (no table) that neither the care arrangement within the couple nor the Use of external care options has a significant effect on career opportunity from fathers has. The influencing factors, the at the knowledge are relevant to employees, career success before starting a family education and the graduating cohort responsible for measuring labor market situation stands.

3.4 Children – career break or career kick?

The Ask after the Meaning the starting a family for the career success in academia, literature has often been overlooked with a view to the private Situation picked up and discussed by female scientists (cf. Lind 2008; Metz-Göckel/Selent/Schuermann 2010; from Stebut 2003). This sub Investigations were largely limited to descriptive accounts of the private circumstances, such as the constellation of partners with regard to qualifications and work area as well as partly the organization of child care. Also, the investigations were mostly either only with quantitative or only examined with qualitative methods and not in their connection function The aim of our contribution was to take up this desideratum and he to investigate, which care strategies scientists with child(ren) with your partners at the persecution of their careers develop and what impact child care solutions have on career opportunities for female scientists.

In the overall view ours findings showed itself, that the family green dung for scientists in the Comparison to your male Colleagues a career disadvantage represents. While Women in the Science before the starting a family just as frequently Success have How Men, takes the Portion from scientists with Success after the birth of first child of away. female scientists the her Career after the starting a family with Success continue, have in the Rule less common and fewer Children, also receive she her first child later as scientists without Career-success. With it becomes the formulated from a life course perspective approach me, that one consolidation the Career before the birth of first child the opportunities for professional Success elevated, confirmed. This on the Behave from Women (or. couples) aiming strategy one late birth might the planning the starting a family to one strong rational Matter. We could show, that this Ask of "right point in time" for the birth of first child for many the female scientists the as well as her profession- wanting to continue a career and having children becomes a burden. female scientists the itself for Children decide, pursue with your partners different strategies, around her employment also after the starting a family to continue. The most interrupt women on-ground from care duties at least for short Time her own professional task. Included showed itself, that the Length of time the interruption through Parents- time the career success the Women after the starting a family co-determined and scientists with short maternity leave in the further career run frequently more successful are as her female colleagues with longer maternity leave. Simultaneously became clearly, that it helpful for scientists is, if them allows becomes, also while the maternity leave Connection at her professional to keep the environment.

As the dominant childcare arrangement after starting a family tion was also found among female scientists in (academic) partner create the traditional gendered division of labour. A specialty tion in the sense of family economic considerations does not apply to the scientists and her partner to, the after the starting a family and also during short career breaks due to parental leave stick to their job steadfastly. An exception is a case with vice versa traditional care arrangement. This is where specialization takes place the partner, who had no career intentions himself, to look after the child and household chores, while his wife scientific career pursued.

A look at the negotiation processes of the couples showed that the traditional tional arrangement is not always the result of conscious decisions and not always "wanted" is. As well as on pages the scientists as
also on the part of their partners there are obstacles that lead to unequal the division of tasks in the partnership. These are, for one unsuccessful negotiations between the scientists and their partners about their respective wishes with regard to the division of labor in children's care and on the other

hand fears that these to enforce without experiencing sanctions. The latter fear became specially formulated for the partners of the female scientists who – if they go on parental leave or reduce working hours for childcare – supposedly larger Disadvantages have as scientists. Out of ver-From an action-theoretical point of view, this results in disadvantages for knowledge female workers, which means that they mostly take care of the children take over. From this it can be concluded that not only the resource relationship between the partners in the negotiation process is crucial. Added come deep-seated normative, gender-differentiated beliefs, as expectations of oneself (as mother/father) and of the partner(s) ner (as father/mother). In processes of inner-partner Scientific *doing gender* puts these expectations into practice and also lead in the case of female scientists, who cite an egalitarian claim formulate their partners, after starting a family to a traditional care arrangement. attributions, that care duties simple to be reconciled with the activity in science than with active abilities in other professional fields, insofar as they are only for work used by female scientists – a gender-differentiated graced division of labour (Hess/Rusconi/Solga 2011a). In partnerships, in where both partners equally take care of tasks, which these attributions deconstruct as gendered attributions ed and the everyday practice of action again and again to the desired equality checked towards.

In principle, female scientists themselves responsibilities, whether they do so in traditional arrangements or in evenly split do with her partner.

scientists with a traditional care arrangement have significantly lower Career opportunities than those who take care of their responsibilities partners at least share equally. For those scientists who, despite traditional arrangements, pursue their careers after starting a family can continue, *flexible* outsourcing of childcare a central role. Female scientists achieve this flexibility by providing care facilities *and* private individuals for care combine your child. Childcare outsourcing and Combination of different third persons or entities is total quite a pre-requisite care solution. It is required that corresponding opportunities for external support on site in sufficient the Availability consist. Also is decisive, if the use this support options by the scientists can be financed. Especially during the doctoral phase, scientists have a low income and are therefore in the financing external limited care options. The possibility of a free support from a personal network such as family members ge or friends can be helpful and correspondingly higher costs for the care of the child by childminders, babysitters or caregivers directions – but not all scientists can do so access such a private network.

The reliable and independent assumption of childcare ung by the partner therefore represents a relief for the women who Childcare by third parties is difficult to replace. To ensure this the partners of the female scientists not only have to orientation of their partners ideally, but above all practically supported Zen. The qualitative evaluations also showed that the professional and partnership satisfaction is particularly high among couples who itself the care of common children share equally.

Our Results throw Questions for further Research on. for There is a need for research, for example, when examining career conditions ments that emanate from the old and the new federal states. Because in The literature showed an astonishing difference in the proportion of professors run, the Children have. Here permit itself numerous Questions connect: Possibly do women at universities in the new federal states better career opportunities than in the old federal states?

shape east german cal scientists the division of care work more egalitarian than west german? Which role play here couple arrangements and external Care for the career opportunities from scientists in the Comparisonto them in the old federal states?

In addition, it would be about the compatibility of family and science interesting not only to look at those women who have remained successfully in science, but also the "exit clot". In this way, barriers for women dealing with their private situation could be eliminated related, determine even more clearly. The problem is all However, in the identification and accessibility of the dropouts, because they go in the Qualification process lost.

A further Point, at to the the Research to career histories fromwomen in science, the timing of the family founding. It would be worth investigating more closely whether starting a family before the first academic degree is positive tively affects the career success of women. This speaks against the Assuming from a life course perspective, yet one can be so sooner time of starting a family can certainly be associated with advantages. The child is then, if the Requirements the qualification phase particularly are high, as with the doctorate and habilitation, in a less supervised intensive age. Under the current conditions of almost without taking temporary occupation in the science system stands this consideration however the (professional) planning uncertainties from boys scientists and their partners.

4. "Under pressure ...!?" - Biographical Orientations of female scientistsin Profession, partnership and Family

For it is exceedingly daring for a young scholar who has no fortune has to expose himself to the conditions of an academic career at all. He must be able to endure at least a number of years without knowing in any way whether he afterwards has a chance of moving into a position sufficient for subsistence" (Weber 1992 [1919]:72).

Even if the young scholar mentioned above - thanks to the opening of the schools for women – meanwhile more and more often also *the* young scholars Weber's description of being a scientist almost has it hundred years later still topical: after a phase of socialization tion the universities and of Professional of scientist in the center of

20th century (cf. Mittelstraß 2006) the situation of many scientific lers and scientists in the present through precarious career and marked living conditions. This precarity complicated by a height uncertainty in the Occupation, longing qualification phases and varying gradient pattern many times the Career- and life planning the affected persons and their partners. The organization University functions included after How before as "reading apparatus" (see. Weber 1992 [1919]). Compared to the many doctorates and habilitation tion, there are only a few permanent positions in the academic system (cf. Engler 2003). The scientific career thus remains open to all science schaftler and scientists one risky and deprived Company on the way to a professorship (cf. Kahlert 2010). But how- Furthermore, scientific careers represent a special biographical cal risk, and what is the importance of work, partnership and Family one?

The aim of this article is to provide professional orientation for women in the Science in the interplay of familial and institutional events sen and to examine their importance for career progression in more detail determine.

For this purpose, problem-centered qualitative interviews with academic learn and interviews with your life partners social science- hermeneutic evaluated. It became the career histories from Knowledge- reconstructed on the basis of their (self-)descriptions and with the partner's perspective on women's professional activities added. The present case descriptions show how the knowledge schaftler in important professional or family decisions orient themselves and to what extent their professional and life courses through lungs with to the partner or through institutional predetermined professional opportunities are affected. The institution of higher education with its specific corresponding organizational structure represents an important con- text knowledge for the interpretation of the self-reports of scientists to represent. Hereinafter becomes for this reason the science system with its institutional and symbolic Order on the basis of for level described. In the center of contribution stand selected Case descriptions and a comparative discussion of the shaft and institutional occasions different professionalorientations the Women in the Science. The empirical analysis shows how women and their partners anticipate and how they integrate them into their joint career and life plans include.

4.1 "Under pressure ...!?" - Women in science

The small number of female professors at universities indicates that that the scientific system is not a gender-neutral place and the organizations nization of the selection of (young) scientists are not independent of gender (cf. e.g. Acker 1990; Hess/ Rusconi/Solga 2011a; Krais 2000; Zimmer/Krimmer/Stallmann 2007). science Female scientists are more subject to selection than their male colleagues tion processes on the way to the professorship and have clearly lesser Opportunities for men to remain permanently in science (cf. Metz Goeckel/Selent/Schuermann 2010; Solga/Stake 2009).

When they are employed at universities or research institutes are scientists with a wide range of work and Challenges for advancement, as they are in research and teaching as well as professional culture. Due to gendered organizations structures (cf. Acker 1990), the universities of Frau- Men and women rate professional achievements differently tet (cf. Beaufaÿs 2003, 2004; Krais 2000). The resulting unequal che professional positioning from Women and men in the Science

"Under pressure ...!?" Biographical orientations from scientists 119

has already been the subject of numerous investigations (see, inter alia, Hess/Rusconi/ Solga 2011a; Matthies 2006; Solga/Pahl 2009; Zimmer/Krimmer/Stallmann 2007). The professional and family orientations of scientists and female scientists on the way to a professorship, however, are hardly researched. So is largely unknown, How scientists the in the Career and life course addressed to them, some of which are contradictory Work on and process the requirements of work and partnership biographically and which Meaning her professional orientation for selection processes in the has career history.

How young scientists use their career opportunities cen at universities and non-university research institutions estimate, shows a standardized study in which, taking into account higher-level goals in life, the professional orientation of the scientific scientific offspring were worked out (cf. Jaksztat/Schinder/ Briedis 2010). Although the scientific work of many respondents is described as attractive, there is in particular the desire for a professional Security with the lack of plannability of scientific careers, the low job security and uncertain opportunities for advancement within the scientific system (Jaksztat/Schinder/ Briedis 2010: 27f.). The longer dwell time in the science system promotes the pessimistic attitude of all scientists tables assessment the own career perspective, ie PhD assess their prospects significantly more negatively than

doctoral students (Jaksztat/ Schinder/Briedis 2010: 30).

For the question of interest here about the (self-)selection processes in science it is significant that scientists and scientists in particular female employees with a pronounced advancement orientation their professional do not see the possibilities within science very positively and half consider leaving science (Jaksztat/Schinder/Briedis 2010: 25f.). With regard to one's own professional situation, professional and Goals in life particularly diverge when it comes to compatibility from family life planning and professional Requirements goes. The Differentiation by gender also shows that men choose their career opportunities within and above all outside of the science system ver than women (Jaksztat/Schinder/Briedis 2010: 29).

Because of the precarious Conditions of Employment become Knowledge- schaftler and scientists also without the Security, that her effort leads to a permanent position in the structure of the university encouraged to see themselves as "scientific self-entrepreneurs" and constantly tinkering with their careers (Enders 2003: 256). At the same time scientific work is accompanied by an ethos that provides that the Science to the "Vocation", ie to one life form becomes. "Naturally, I live only for think ‚Profession'" may be – Max weaver (1992 [1919]: 80) according to the answer expected of a young scholar. The term Appointment implies that the everyday life of a scientist or a scientist scientist "is cleansed of everything that is not related to science and contains everything that is useful for its operation" (Beaufaÿs 2004: para. 5). Unlike in the days of Max Weber, there have been higher education institutions in the 1960s and 1970s increasingly female che scholars who pursue a scientific career after graduating from university begin. But can straight female scientists there she mostly with equally highly qualified and full-time employed partners men are (cf. Hess/Rusconi/Solga 2011a; Rusconi/Solga 2008), their everyday life seldom keep them free from everything extra-professional than their male ones colleagues possible is (cf. Chapter 3 in this A book).

If in the analysis from career histories in the Science soalso the private living conditions of scientists and scientific learners, ie their partnerships and families, are included the discussion about vocations and precariousness, especially for women additional explosiveness. Then Gender has furthermore one structuring Effect in the lives of women and men. It attacks both on the plane societal and social expectations as well as at the institutional level tuitions and organizations regulate people's lives (cf. Krueger 2002). To all events specific to the course of life, such as entry in working life or the birth of children, a set of ties Behaviors that are standardized by gender. These take flow to individual biographical actions as well as interactive acts in pairs and are partly reproduced here. That's how it is explained for example, that even groups of people with strong professional ambitions tion - such as highly qualified couples who start out as professional equals - in the In the course of starting a family, a re-traditionalization of their division of labor subject in the couple relationship and on one, namely the male carriere (cf. chapter 2 in this book;

Bathmann/Müller/Cornelißen 2011; Wimbauer et al. 2008).

How far scientists and their life partners their professional Organizing careers together or separately depends on many different which factors (cf. Behnke/Meuser 2003). In heterosexual partners are mostly women – even if they are (fully) employed – for childcare and so-called "compatibility management" responsible (see Chapter 3 in this book; Behnke/Meuser 2005; Hess/Rusco- not 2010). Analyzes have been carried out with regard to the assumption of childcare but shown that partners who take responsibility for the care of the common same children take over, female scientists focus on theirs professional enable development (cf. Chapter 3 in this A book).

Whether and to what extent highly qualified couples requirements, with those particularly Women in the life course confronted *Under pressure ...!?" Biographical orientations from scientists* 121

anticipate and incorporate them into the joint career and life planning related, has been little researched so far. Taking into account the above mentioned observation of a "socialization" of science is in With regard to previous research results to take into account that at scientist and scientists directed Expectations of "self-entrepreneurship" frequently in couple relationships designed become. This raises the question of the tension between organization and partnership is traded. It could e.g. B. be that partners and partners women in view of the loss of autonomy in the professional activities of scientists an increasingly large part of the motivate those involved. What forms of division of labor which couples incorporate is still unknown. It would be possible that Partners are increasingly taking on tasks that used to be more "functional" pairings (e.g. by sponsors in science). became. Couple relationships would therefore not only be seen as intimate part- nerships to understand, rather also as scientific (professional) partnerships in the senses from mutual content and more strategicAdvice. [1]

"

4.2 *Career orientations of female scientists (case descriptions)*

In the case descriptions, supplemented by the perspective of their partner, who present the professional and personal histories of four female scientists were asked who had an academic career at the time of the interview. [2] It is worked out which biographical, partnership and institutional factors on the professional orientations from successful women working in science.

4.2.1 *methodical Proceed*

The basis for the Investigation place the in the Frame of project
"Making a career together" qualitative interviews with knowledge workers and their partners. There were total 33 Science-

---

[1] The validity of this assumption would be an additional explanation for the relative career advantage from female scientists whose partner also as scientist employed are (see. Hess/Rusconi/Solga 2011a).
The term scientific career indicates that the women are in an age- and qualification- cation adequate occupation condition. To the in the Project "Together Career make" developed standardized career definition see. Chapter 1 in this A book. students who were at different career stages in qualitative ones interviews and twelve of their partners. The interviewees of qualitative sub study became out of the participants and participants the standardized survey selected (please refer Chapter 1 in this A book).

The qualitative sample consists of scientists from the three dis- ziplining (social, technical and natural sciences), career stages and pair Career constellations together, which due to the standardized were known during the survey and were used for case selection. This combination sizing does not correspond to statistical representativeness, but follows the methodological considerations of the "theoretical sampling" of the Grounded theory (cf. Glaser/Strauss 1967). This makes it possible, among other things, according to the socio-scientific-hermeneutical evaluation with far-reaching to work with case variations (cf. Reichertz/Schröer 1994), e.g. B. regarding Age, number of children and involvement of partners in childcare Hungarian

The scientists were trained in problem-centered, process-structured ated interviews on individual episodes of their professional and partnership biography questioned (see. joke 2000). Included became Inquire flexible handled to the willingness for a comprehensive biographical narrative to increase (cf. Hopf 1978; Schütze 1984). The interviews took place in the Usually at respondents' place of work or at one chosen by them Location instead of and lasted about two Hours.

The transcribed interviews became first content analytical and evaluated in a comparative way (cf. Mayring 2003) in order to quantities in a first step. In the course of content analysis The comparison of topics became both theory-led and text-based The interview transcripts were coded. This allowed the to bundle self-declarations of the interviewees thematically and relevant key categories for a cross-case view of subjective knowledge of scientists about their professional careers identify. outgoing from exemplary cases became then inter selected view passages for a sequence analysis evaluation and inter- (cf. Hitzler/Honer 1997; Oevermann et al. 1979). The generated case-related findings are presented here.

In order to specifically emphasize the importance of the biographical orientations of the To show women in the field of tension between university and partnership, certain characteristics were kept relatively stable for the present analysisten: At the time of the interview, the four scientists presented here punkt about 40 years old and live in existing for more than ten years partnerships; three of them with children. All four scientists realize with Success one Career; two from they are professors. Three of the life partners also work as scientists, partly in the same Area of Expertise. A life partner is in the the same Area of Expertise outside of the *Under pressure ...!?" Biographical orientations from scientists* 123

science active. Three of the four couples realize a double career at fourth couple, only the woman has a career in the sense of the defined career definition. Despite the professional success of everyone responsible for this wear chosen cases differentiate itself career histories and food situations the scientists partially strong from each other. In addition two of the cases indicate a dominance of vocational orientation and two for a dominance of family orientation (see Figure 4.1). On In this way, the field of tension between institutional and partner- more scientific Support contrasting certainly become. The Goal the Case descriptions is the interrelationship of professional action and partnership and institutional context in the self-declaration ten the show female scientists.

A short description of the cases with information on professional and partner course as well as to the social structure the parental homes located itself in Section 4.5 (Attachment of this chapter).

4.2.2 *To the Science appointed (Case 1: Behrendt)*

The first case presented here is an example of a scientist who lives with an equally successful scientist and in whose partnership the family responsibilities (gender) atypical distributed are (please refer Section 4.5.1). The career orientation from Woman Behrendt is on science as a vocation and as a career.

"I think I have more will to power or something. So I am, [...] I'm going always right in the middle of all these stories, like bodies and whatever. take all possible invitations within the institutions in which I work and such further. Get bogged down in this too, and so on. But my significant other is stronger focussed and concentrated. [...] We were both already quite calibrated, that we wanted to do this, to work in science. In my case even more than with him with no alternative. I [...] could do it then and I can do it now always still not introduce, What I otherwise do could. So also really from the Can here. [...] I think, we had both at that time, believe I, not said, that we just so end up. [...] But for me was for example professor become nothing unimaginable."

The professional actions of Ms. Behrendt are characterized by a habitual scientific professionalism, which comes with a the ability to achieve professional goals. According to the condition" of their family of origin, the already several generations professed sors out brought has, takes she no professional alternatives true. She follows her chosen path into science and does not explicitly describe the professorship as a professional goal, but addresses it with greater matter of course the in of their biography undertaken steps toward it. Hurdles raised by other respondents, such as a longer financial precariousness or the impertinence, despite having a family geographically Being mobile doesn't seem to matter to Ms. Behrendt. decision

Applications for job offers are largely determined by your individual professional ches advancement determines what, in case of doubt, a spatial separation from the partner requires. Woman Behrendt understands Science as "Attitude", by that she means job, family and life to the demands of scientific to orient towards a professional career. It thus corresponds to the research literature describes the passionate scientist who those with the "devotion" of the whole described at the beginning of the chapter person for science lives (cf. Beaufaÿs 2004).

In addition to the habitual professionalism, the professional action of Woman Behrendt also through one orientation on influence marked draws. She has a sense for positions of power and therefore brings herself- half in the strategic decision-making bodies of the institutions, for which she works. Offers addressed to you, e.g. B. Invitations to lectures or participation in committees, she rarely refuses. This procedure refers to them as "going in the middle"; it enables Ms. Behrendt to to keep track of the course of their professional development. the up building and maintaining their scientific networks are just as important their career planning as well as the applications for positions that are of interest to them. The action orientation of Ms. Behrendt thus moves in the span voltage field between one high matter of course and one Above- shot of professional activity - which means that Ms. Behrendt die individual steps of their professional career with big Success accomplished.

"Under pressure ...!?" Biographical orientations from scientists 125

At the same time, it becomes clear that they cannot pursue their career path without the support tongue other people realized:

"So I am quite secure, that really without this persons and through the, What she to me and also have made possible for others, and structures that they have created at the universities, How graduate schools and so further, the not possible been were. So it was repeated several times at different points, so to speak, [...] that I very supports been am. So the is quite secure the somehow most important. [...] And the other just as important or very important, [...] also a partner for whom it is absolutely self-evident that we both have scientific careers ren make and that the not on Costs from something other goes. So that we the both not so see, that it is called, then can man something other not or so, rather with same attitude do science."

A good institutional connection enables Ms. Behrendt, throughout since the doctorate in a close network of supporters and supporters to work for women, from whom she receives a lot of support and also as a important driver for their professional development. In addition, she receives plenty of freedom in their jobs to implement their own research ideas zen and build up your own research profile. She works from the promotion tion to positions with rather longer-term contracts, which you at least for offer a perspective for a few years. Ms. Beh- yields for their entire professional development.

Ms. Behrendt also receives support and advice in her partnership. There her partner also as scientist employed is and the requirements of the scientific profession is the exchange about the professional Field an important part of the couple's regular conversations and a more supportive factor in the individual career planning of women Behrendt. Mister Behrendt is a more equal Partner, the itself above also primarily responsible for childcare for long periods of time takes care. The couple negotiates the family work needs-based. Woman Behrendt is a little older than her partner, which she sees as an advantage. She is the first in the relationship to complete her studies and qualification work ten and then, with her appointment as a professor, lays down the permanent liable for family residence. 3

By both partners sharing their professional goals with each other and each other support each other in their professional ambitions, the couple in the Behrendt case to Wissenschaft as a "joint venture" at. Despite the same goals, Ms. Behrendt claims in her self-description practice a different career strategy for themselves than for their partner. in delimitation tongue to of their own power orientation describes she your partner as

---

3 However, in her self-description, the latter is not only described as supportive, but also described as a loss of spatial and temporal flexibility. She justifies this by saying that the common domicile of the family is relocated to their place of work and that all day-to-day responsibility for the concerns of the children falls to Ms. Behrendt, while this before her partner essential accepted has.

more motivated in terms of content and with a professional interest in To become a specialist in your field. These different, themselves mutually complementary career strategies are what are in the description Ms. Behrendt's practice enables both of them to continue their professional activities to pursue with success; that the content focus of the partner luckily one consequence out of the special dynamics of couple is,remains included disregarded.

Mr. Behrendt, who keeps an eye on family cohesion, fits his job search to the circumstances created by Mrs. Behrendt. He partially restricts himself when looking for a job and chooses his professional ones Opportunities so that the family can continue. The partner opened on this Way a free space for Woman Behrendt, in to the she seemingly carefree in the interest hers professional progress act,interesting Place assume and particular status positions to reach can. The fact that both partners "pull in the same direction" is ten imbalance, the after years Expression in Woman Behrendts

finds "a bad conscience", [4] it is clear that Mr. Behrendt in relation expresses no dissatisfaction with his own professional career. Open- he obviously does not understand his own professional development in competition to that of his partner and, looking back, doesn't have the feeling technically to have renounced special professional opportunities. Ms. Beh yields and her partner prove itself with it as *professionally complementary* , the manage it despite institutional conditions requiring flexibility, a Equal partnerships based on the professional success of both partners to lead society and a double career - also in the romantic sense realize.

Although Woman Behrendt and her partner as well as in the professional as also achieve a high level of satisfaction in the private sphere also with them "limits of feasibility". Years of commuting is ahead especially a burden when the time for the family is very scarce and is no longer regularly available due to excessive distances. To- it becomes clear that a life – like that of the Behrendt couple – is one very high logistical and planning effort required. Again and again It is checked and agreed whether and to what extent both partners (and the children) feel comfortable in the current situation and how it is professionally and with of the family goes on. The frequent communicative exchange leads to that it one height accordance in the interpretations from Woman and Mr

---

4 Ms. Behrendt would actually like to have an equal partnership in which both partners can realize themselves professionally and take on responsibility for the family men. Theoretically, she does not want to curtail her partner's professional freedom and relieve him of family chores. In fact, however, Mr. Behrendt is already taking over early after the birth of the first child more responsibilities related to the family and carries over many Years the primary responsibility for the care and education of Children.

"Under pressure ...!?" Biographical orientations from scientists 127

Behrendt regarding the life together. This is with the others do not mate consistently the case.

4.2.3 *In small steps after above (Case 2: pointer)*

The second case presented is similar to the Behrendt case for a science senschaftler who shares her professional life with her in the Science make partner tracked (please refer Section 4.5.2). In the In contrast to the first case, Ms. Zeiher and her partner have no children. Woman Zeihers professional orientation directs itself alone on Science as

"Calling" - she sees herself as a person dedicated solely to the content of a profession and not for his status interested.

"It just happened because it's just a career. [...] For me it wasn't now the goal of becoming a professor at some point... I just wanted to continue researching. [...] It was particularly important that you always worked very diligently both during the doctorate and was also during the postdoc position and had as a goal, but in research remain. I tried to acquire third-party funds myself [...], so first the postdoc Job out of think own grants, and also the habilitation position actually."

Ms. Zeiher's action orientation can best be described as "Politics of small steps". Without a professorship as the goal right from the start in mind, Ms. Zeiher plans her professional development step-by-step way. While she on one position is, has she the next stage alreadyin the eye. Your professional orientation is not based on prestige certain positions, but in the permanent change and improvement of their own professional position. The professional actions of Ms. Zeiher is highly adaptable to the requirements and character of the science system. She knows its principle pien exactly and describes himself as hardworking and goal-oriented. To their Career planning involves a lot of personal initiative. She always applies in good time tig and to several places at the same time. In her applications she is very flexible. Ms Zeiher creates her own jobs several times, by submitting applications for their own projects and using the funds they have raised her own position is also financed with her own funds. your passion for Content of their activity is in their self-interpretation of the reason why it it does not require any strength to overcome, in terms of the requirements and performance gene one science career Exactly "correct" to act. Woman pointer receives the central motivation for the development of their career exclusively lich out of their content interest and not, How Woman Behrendt, also by reaching decision positions. Your representation of scientific career as a "career" implies that in a way they don't have any another choice has than to rise to the rank of professor.

Against the background that she is already a professor, she works in her Self-description as a person "who just wants to keep doing research" relatively modest. This self-description is not accidental: As educational climber, she does not start her career with the same natural matter of course like Ms. Behrendt. In order not to take any risks hen and possibly without Offer to stand by developed itself Woman pointer early to the entrepreneur of their Self and funded all her Positions up to a professorship on raising research funds. For Ms. Zeiher considers it a central motive in employment to work in which they are relatively independent of superiors can.

In this professional activity, Ms. Zeiher corresponds almost completely to an image of the scientist as a self-entrepreneur, to which the increasing science system geared towards efficiency and competition. cut is: a self-reliant and adaptable person son, which conducts third-party funded, project-related research. Simultaneously Ms. Zeiher's origin-related modesty becomes necessary Strategy. Unlike Ms. Behrendt, Ms. Zeiher doesn't show anyone on the outside will to power. She does not claim ascension or influence to want to take - behavioral characteristics that are more likely to be granted to men become. Mrs. Zeiher remains modest towards her colleagues and is equivalent to with it the expected "feminine" connoted behavioral to paint. This withdrawal of content may be necessary in order to within the male-dominated field of natural sciences, rose to secure as a scientist.

Ms. Zeiher's career path is characterized by a succession of different different occupations in which they do the research that is of interest to them can realize. Already at the beginning of her career and later she has sponsors and colleagues who she in their venture and to whom they have a close social keeps in touch. Right at the start of your career, during your doctorate, her doctoral supervisor encourages her to do so by going abroad to make more independent. But what she benefits most from is the expertise hers older partners. This advises she as expert one similar for research field in terms of content and strategy.

"Nevertheless, I think it was more comfortable for me that he was a step ahead was. But that also means that you have the disadvantage that you almost never live on a world length is, in fact. But still, [...] probably it was pretty stimulating too- ren. [...] He also gave me tremendous support in [...] writing motions. He has [...] supported me and said [...] that one could try to get a habilitation position receive, and as I said, but to apply for the position yourself."

Ms. Zeiher is the close interlocking of couple relationships and gainful employment through her own Parents trusted. The Parents – without academic final se – have worked very closely together for many years and right in the Profession supports. In the Difference in addition pursue however Woman and Mister pointer individual professional Goals. The mutual Support aims to make it possible to achieve one's own goals. Mister Zeiher, who at the beginning of the couple's relationship already had a major career sprung is not only a partner and colleague for Ms. Zeiher, but also role model and mentor. His successful career shows her exemplary ways for her own professional development and offers Mrs. Zeiher Orientation. She benefits from the expertise of her partner, who a very similar field of research in their content and career replanning work to Page stands. With her appointment as a professor Ms. Zeiher catches up professionally with her partner; marked them a turning point in Relationship of professional positions of the couple.

The couple takes many to realize their individual professional goals Phases of distance relationship in purchase. Larger distances are of both accepted, even if this cuts back on life together as Pair mean. Also the reprieve the starting a family allows the Continuation of individualistic relationship practice. The legitimacy for these clear cuts in private and/or family life is in the Passion with which Ms. Zeiher describes her attitude towards her job. she is the justification and legitimacy for their life outside of work moves into the background. Although Ms. Zeiher has clear ideas about it that she would not make any compromises professionally for the couple relationship de, it becomes clear that life between two cities is not permanent is easy. The enormous amount of work with which both partners on their chairs confronted are, and the wide distance between your respective places of work and residence make commuting "too exhausting" and cause the couple to get together a maximum of three weekends a month sees. By making it clear to both partners that they will only do this for a few years and cannot endure in the long run, the instability of this relationship food arrangements. The Offer hers partners she could at any time out of leaving her job when it "gets too much" is not what a woman does Zeiher wishes. Against the background of her professional advancement rather it is clear that Mr Zeiher sees his wife professionally as his mentee, but not as professional equals. [5] Accordingly, Ms. Zeiher is the nige who states that they are coping with the current situation much better than you partner by trying to get through a reduced number of regular mutual Visit Stability in her relationship to bring.

---

[5] We have seen this form of offers from partners to their wives several times in the views found. Together refer she on a recognition problem the Men across from your professionally successful partners.

4.2.4 *Seek after Security (Case 3: Lehnert)*

In contrast to the first two cases, which indicate dominance in the professional the third case is an example of one orientation at the Goal the compatibility from Profession and Family (please refer Section 4.5.3). The view of science as a vocation receives sem case a different meaning and is accompanied by doubts about the Compatibility of scientific occupation with family, through questions of livelihood and the planning of job and family added.

"It showed me what the great thing about science is. That one his own projects pursue can and simply this incredible Freedom has and basically doing what you enjoy every day. This is an incredibly privi- alloyed work, I find. And it comes at the price of not being able to make ends meet financially secure inside establish can on one quite, quite longing View. And for me possible never. Well, making it to the professorship is not my ambition at all. So I would to me actually always gladly one niche in the central building seek want."

Woman Lehnerts interpretations to the Science as field of activity are from Marked by opposites, manifested as indecisiveness even in her find career history. On the one hand is Mrs. Lehnert from Cha- actor of the scientific work very convinced and describes it as one creative and varied Task, the she very gladly exercises She enjoys the scientific work and especially the substantive She really appreciates the freedom of this job. On the other side, Ms. Lehnert repeatedly remarks that her picture is of a ing activity in addition to the content-creative work also through a ability with family time and lucrative source of income is determined. Ms. Lehnert sees these conditions in the usual employment conditions in science that are on the way to a science map re to graduate are, not fulfilled.

A look at Ms. Lehnert's career shows that both the

initial situation as well as the career path are not designed without obstacles ten. Ms. Lehnert starts as an educational climber with less cultural Capital and already encounters conditions during her doctorate that Started in the scientific Work make more difficult. She PhD on a scholarship, has hardly any contact with her doctoral supervisor and has to ask her finance the third year of the doctorate through work commissions and other work. After completing her doctorate, Ms. Lehnert only receives a one-year contract. The precarious employment situation during and after your doctorate is up to you Need for planning and securing the family and living together with the partner. In anticipation of the forthcoming family During her postdoc period, Ms. Lehnert begins a position outside of of science to seek her regular working hours and long-term employment prospects offer should. The birth of their Children moves the Desire to have time outside of work and financially secure be at the center of their ideas of satisfying work. The location of the activity within or outside of science therefore secondary. Ms. Lehnert's indecision in the professional Orientation is also evident in the years in which they were in a scientific company is employed: She recognizes how important the content-related working as a scientist, and will return after the company is dissolved back to scientific work. Since then she has been on a short sluggish as a part-time employee and would not like to enough to work full-time. The employment relationships will be (Prospective) match to family life selected, with the local and temporal fixations of Working conditions are key.

The professional Act from Woman Lehnert is through this characterizes that she professional occasions seeks and perceives without completely after to want above. Although Mrs. Lehnert feels called to science, marks itself her career path through job change and one certain Indecision. This indecisiveness must also be seen as an *expression of structural precarization* scientific employment relationships understood become. activities on one perpetual Job in part time – how she wishes Ms. Lehnert after the birth of her children - are in science system not intended. Similar How at Woman pointer receives the idea of a scientific vocation has a different meaning for Ms. Lehnert tion: It is limited to the content without both advancement and to want to realize flow taking. Unlike Mrs. Zeiher, she sees however – because of of their orientation on Family and validation – under the given conditions in science, no professional one Future.

"I must honest say, that I the enjoy both to have and also really more having time for the kids. And the part-time position suits me very well. I have sometimes the feeling that my husband has less of a problem with it, now a full-time place to fill in and then to do less of the other things. But he says he would also feel like turning it around, and then I would just do it attempt with the Full time job, if I the get. The is but very unlikely."

After her doctorate and the birth of her children, Mrs. Lehnert begins her transfer some of their professional ambitions to their partner. you con- structures their career as not linear and leaves the goal-oriented directed her pursuit of a professorship to her husband, whom she supports to establish oneself in science in the long term. Two careers in science to realize and have a family, Mrs. Lehnert appears on not possible due to work requirements. Instead, she hopes that her Mann soon a lifetime position as a professor after successful habilitation receives and supports his scientific career by care the Children mostly takes over. There the foreseeable End the fellow job hers partners is approaching and Mister Lehnert has not yet received a reputation Ms. Lehnert has to apply for a full-time job that she does not want employment keep ready around "if necessary" the Family to finance. The Her partner's claim that, in case of doubt, she too is the family breadwinner be can, puts Woman Lehnert since the starting a family strengthened under Print.

The family ideas from Mr Lehnert are through his Parents, the both employed were, shaped and at one equality claim aligned. The difficulties for his professional path are his Woman known because after the birth of the children she "only" works part-time and assumes primary responsibility for care work. The assignment However, he finds the role as the main breadwinner to be a burden because he has his job with to the risk tied together sees, not to get ahead ie no to obtain a professorship. Mr. Lehnert would prefer to reduce the risk to two to distribute people, i.e. him *and* his wife. Using the example of a rejected th job offer to the couple – with five years of employment in the same city – where she got an assistant position in a young group and he would have gotten a lectureship with little research Mr. Lehnert clearly that his wife will take over the main breadwinner role declines. At the same time, he takes on less family work than his own Wife, ie he takes care of the children in exceptional cases or together with his Woman who takes care of all regular appointments. He regrets it, none having taken parental leave and sometimes has difficulties with it to be involved in the care of the children.

Contrary to their claim to act as equals in work and family want, Mrs. and Mr. Lehnert realize a traditional division of tasks, in which Mr. Lehnert is the main breadwinner and Ms. Lehnert is an additional breadwinner carer is. It is very clear that the precarious employment situation of the Lehnert couple, namely that the further professional development of both Partner at the time of the interview is unclear, considered by both to be a heavy burden is felt. The occupational insecurity is transferred to the and expresses itself in the dissatisfaction of both partners with the current due division of roles out of. The Ask, How the Tasks distributed become should, it has not been finally clarified for Ms. and Mr. Lehnert what the relationship food arrangement makes the couple feel insecure.

4.2.5 *recognition in Profession and Family (Case 4: Thiel)*

The fourth case represents a female scientist with a dominant family enorientation, which accepts trade-offs rather than private ones (they see section 4.5.4). She takes full responsibility for her child and assigns a secondary role to their partner in childcare. Professionally is she very successful and is working on one firm Job. Despite Similarities in family orientation, the case differs in different different aspects of Ms. Lehnert: This is how Ms. Thiel will functional guarantees possible to shorten their working hours in the long term and self-determined with regard to the compatibility of work and family is correct to be flexible.

"I always have the feeling that I can't finish everything here the way I can would like, and at home exactly the same. It's important that you accept that yourself and that you set priorities. My priority is family and mine Child. And as long as I do my things properly here and have the impression that the big picture is correct and my student employees are also developing and get along with their work, then that's okay too. I have to I myself then keep rethinking and making compromises. [...] Professionally. swabs professionally, Private I would no swabs make."

Ms. Thiel values her work as a scientist very much. in the topic ment of her professional ambitions, Ms. Thiel presents the content of the respective gene projects and positions as well as the scope for independent research to the foreground. Science offers Ms. Thiel a professional field in which she finds fulfillment, but also respect. The latter is tight for them the attainment of certain positions and titles. Although her Career progression through a virtually uninterrupted employment in science distinguished, Ms. Thiel did not pursue the goal from the outset of able to stay. At the beginning of her career she works for a few months in a private company. The decision to Promotion was also pushed by her partner. Mr. Thiel – himself a doctor torand, when the two become a couple - encourages Ms. Thiel to her advance dissertation. The reasons, subsequent to another high- Changing schools and starting your habilitation there will not further discussed; but the decision, the commenced habilitation despite delays through family related interruptions and of bill of exchange on one perpetual Job at her subject area to end. There she fears that her position as academic councilor will result in too much work having to exercise under their qualification ("secretary duties"), the she from fulfilling Work keep hopes she through the To reach the Habilitation later appointed honorary professor at her university become.

"So z. B. the habilitation does not have to be completed in 2011 or 2012, but other then it will be 2014 or completed in 2015."

Ms. Thiel's professional actions are in comparison to the other cases len through one serenity marked. She sees of their professional Looking forward to the future carefree, giving itself plenty of time to complete its habilitation thesis and uses the possibilities of reducing working hours, to devote even more to her child and to get out of micropolitical institute matters pull out. Despite hers gapless career path raises Ms. Thiel does not claim to be single-minded. In the center of There is no description of her employment, as is the case with Ms. Lehnert, who earning money or securing family; in connection with professional For them, self-realization stands for values such as independence and acceptance of responsibility.

Ms. Thiel's composure in career planning can be

seen to the institutional and partnership context in which their professional history is embedded, understand. The institutional context in which Ms Thiel completes her professional development is characterized on the one hand due to the good integration into the institute, the positions with comparatively long contract periods and the many years of support from their doctor torvater, who encourages you early on to set your own research priorities, and she also after the promotion furthermore professional and strategically advises. Ever since she was a child, her absence among colleagues was seen as a lack she knows the value of her work. She appreciates hers substantive contribution to the department as important and irreplaceable. The professional conditions of technical sciences in which employee are generally well equipped, allow Ms. Thiel, overall two years of parental leave without losing their professional status to fear.

In her partnership, too, Ms. Thiel is informed on several levels. supports: On the one hand pulls the partner at your location and look for there a new job; on the other hand he can them due to the same professional qualifications. The consistently high income men from Mr. Thiel represents a safeguard for Ms. Thiel. On a other level, with child care, Ms. Thiel declines the support her partner, on the other hand. She claims this task for herself alone established with her partner after the birth of their child conservative relationship model in which the distribution of tasks between the parents is traditionally justified in terms of gender. Mrs. Thiel describes the Profession hers partners the in the private sector employed is, as the one Employment that is not compatible with childcare responsibilities leaves, ie should not be interrupted for a parental leave because his Gainful employment brings more income and, moreover, also for the everyday Care (because of one low working time flexibility) only very restricted compatible is.

In total meets Woman Thiel the large part the decisions within the family. She organizes and takes care of the children herself Primary responsibility for the common child. This traditional family model is due to the flexible working hours available to her allows. Mister Thiel becomes with it simultaneously as "breadwinner" con- structured. His ambitions, itself out of Found the job dissatisfaction in the first age of child also at the parenting time to participate, who-

that of Ms. Thiel rejected. Mr. Thiel, who manure path also in the engineering sciences PhD has, is in dissatisfied with his current job in the private sector. His current He describes the current job situation as very stressful and he always plays along the thought of resigning from the position. However, he does not report concrete reorientations or exit attempts. Similar it behaves concerned with his involvement in the family and caregiving responsibilities he only at his wife's request. He didn't take parental leave works full time and works overtime – in usually he is not before 19 clock at home. Although he criticizes the traditional division of tasks, it is but not an active option for Ms. Thiel. The relationship between Mr and Woman Thiel is in total through one *complementary asymmetry* marked draws; ie with all statements about her partner underlines Mrs. Thiel the difference to yourself (and vice versa).

taken together proves itself Woman Thiel as clever Manager, the it creates itself not only professionally using their colleagues, but also organize a support network privately through her partner that supports her life choices. The appreciation of their work prompts her colleagues, she in all her desires for more flexible to support working hours and longer breaks due to parental leave Zen. In terms of asymmetric complementarity, it secures itself via the Care hers child recognition and Support hers partners. Unlike Ms. Behrendt, Ms. Thiel does not allow her partner to be active integration in the Childcare, rather transmits him only the Abandonment of financial security as family breadwinner. the difficult things before them too Ms. Thiel repeatedly asked in the course of her career from the birth of her child, she copes with a clear set of priorities tongue. Her strong family orientation leads her to focus professionally on the to concentrate on the most important things - which you can successful.

4.3   Science between Profession and vocation

The case reports, the in the following comparative discussed become, show the widely varying career orientations of female scientists and point to a different weighting of gainful employment and family life by the respondents. In the self-descriptions clear that the scientific ethos mentioned in the introduction is still effective and the professional actions of female scientists ne guides. All four scientists address an inner function to the Science, however understand she underneath different content te, attitudes and working methods, as the following illustration shows (one Summary the respective professional and family orientation finds itself in Figure 4.2).

The reconstruction of career orientation and the behavior of the Scientists Ms. Behrendt and Ms. Zeiher comes in terms of content the meaning of vocation elaborated by Beaufaÿs (2004). In the In the first case, the origin of the scientist favors a career orientation designation, the with a professional attitude and self-image of science as a vocation and the single-minded pursuit of own career and an emancipated understanding of roles in relation to family work easier. In the second case, the focus is on the knowledge senschaft as a vocation with the aim of equal status with the older, scientific successful partner along. Both scientists are very involved in their professional advancement (e.g. through numerous research proposals) and feel called to scientific work. However, both have special conditions that make it possible for them chen, the scientific profession as vocation to live.

In the first case, the high commitment of the partner in the family work to ensure that Ms. Behrendt's everyday work actually of everything that does not directly serve professional advancement, "freely nigt" (Beaufaÿs 2004: para. 5). The partner enables Mrs.

Behrendt to devote themselves to their profession in the same way as their professional orientation corresponds without having to do without a family. These different remember the career strategies of Ms. Behrendt and her partner – with Exception to the assignment of gender - also to the distinction various career strategies by Bock and De Jong (1994; cited by van Doorne-Huiskes/den Dulk/Peper 2005: 50f.). Woman's career strategy Behrendt corresponds to a "career strategy" with which De Jong strives a full-time job, seizing opportunities, ambition, initi- active action and making one's own abilities visible. This Strategy implies that a certain freedom for one's own career is ben, as is more common in men. The career strategy of Mr. Behrendt, on the other hand, shows signs of a "professional strategy". ing, i.e. a stronger focus on content and a lower level of resses on organizational tasks of everyday working life. partnership model le, which enable a strong professional orientation, were gainful for a long time make men Reserved and find itself under female scientists especially if they have children, even today it is still rare (cf. Hess/ Rusconi 2010).

In the second case, too, the scientist follows me an exclusive focus on her job. She poses with rising the success of the profession through the partnership and moves together with her Partner, the also as professor employed is, the founding one family love As a self-entrepreneur, Ms. Zeiher makes for her professional Success is self-responsible and suits her actions in the private sphere as well to the professional requirements. Childlessness as a strategy for or as The consequence of professional success is already inherent in science constantly discussed (e.g. Chapter 3 in this book; cf. Metz-Göckel/ Möller/Auferkorte-Michaelis 2009).

Although the "inner" vocation to science also includes self-description exercises of the other two scientists, their dedication to the job through the family orientation, the everyday actions and the orientation focus on securing their families is significantly restricted. So knows Although Ms. Lehnert is very interested in the content, the contradictions between the demands of the scientific profession and the Desire for family lead to the interviewee summing up, division of labour only one person can make a career in science. Through the traditional understanding of the couple's role, the lot falls on the partners who are further along in their careers. In the fourth case, the University for the scientist represents a professional field in which they can pursue substantive interests and that they with their family life, the plays a central role, can be reconciled very well. The existing near Career- and status orientation is closely with the facts ver- that a secure income (permanent position) is only possible in high positions le) can be achieved. Both scientists see in the scientific a job that they practice in addition to other aspects of their lives can. To her professional understanding heard also the clear limitation the Working hours, ie part-time work. Due to the better contractual conditions, the possibility of self-determined work and ultimately also the permanent position, Ms. Thiel experiences her work as a scientist as compatible with your aim in others Areas of life. Woman Lehnert,those due to the time-limited contracts and the collaboration in projects is under much more pressure, sees her expectations of science shaft as Profession, the the compatibility with other goals in life, fewer met as Ms. Thiel.

Since all four interviewees had professional successful, but not all four women already have a reputation as pro- receive a professorship or a secure position within the science system tems, despite the differences in professional orientation tion and the design of career paths do not make up exactly what che orientation supposedly "better" for the successful graduate a science career. Orientations in work and family are narrowintertwined with the institutional and partnership framework and guide the professional and family activities of female scientists call. In the case of Ms. Lehnert, it was clearly shown that after the birth of the children more strongly on the reconciliation of family and career The scientist directed orientation in the sense of self-selection has caused certain job offers to be rejected and the partner the career-oriented Goals to transfer. Here becomes the professional Even- given up with the partner for family life: the asked scientist changing from science to business, then back to part-time science to take primary responsibility for adopting children in the traditional family model. This family orientation is closely linked to your professional orientation and is not different: The scientist does not look for the institutional planned position of an interesting postdoc job as a half, but fixed Job. The science system sees a "half/n Researcher" does not propose, which is why she tries to find her professional orientation in science society by withdrawing its own claims. The opposite may be due to professional orientation adjustments in the family area. These adaptations see family changes Forms of life, as in the case of Mrs. Behrendt, because of her job does not live in the same place with her partner, or as in the case of Ms Zeiher, who does not start her own family because of her professional goals. the professional Orientation before and during the phase of starting a family and the Ask after the professional Security after the family phase are with itan important influencing factor for the academic career (cf. also Chapter 3 in this A book).

When comparing the career orientations of female scientists in addition on, that one fixed and clear anchoring in the Science,
who are in continuous employment as scientific

employees beiterin puts it, leads to a different assessment of one's own chances as a through grants or Unemployment interrupted career. Are offered as a long-term loose connection to a department Scholarship holder no or only very short employment after the doctorate relationships becomes one college career as incompatible with the professional and life goals assessed. So can insecure, unsupportive Framework conditions as in the case of Ms. Lehnert to change the professional and/or family orientation. Here it shows that the difficult starting conditions of their scientific career despite high intrinsic motivation to temporarily turn away from the science system tem can lead. The scientist, who at the beginning who have fewer obstacles to overcome in their professional careers, work closely with mentors and mentors or other supporters together men work, in the course of the career an ever stronger career orientation, ie a will to rise. This is how Ms. Thiel will increasingly important to have a position that is appropriate to their qualifications to take on, on which it receives recognition. This causes them to that despite her permanent position as an academic councillor, she is completing her habilitation conclude and would like to be promoted to professor.

Compares man the career paths the scientists with those of their partners, it is also noticeable that the partners usually have longer relationships have sluggish and continuous employment relationships and certainly more optimistic on her professional Future in the Science look, although they also partly address uncertainties caused by short contracts This largely corresponds to the above-mentioned by Jaksztat, Schin-Der and Briedis (2010) worked out findings on gender differences divorced the assessment of career opportunities in the Science.

4.4 *Summary and outlook*

The present Contribution visualized the special Meaning the equal design the couple relationship for the realization more successful career paths from scientists and might clearly to what extent the institution college careers by women can promote.

As a rule, the female scientists understand each other compared to theirs partners as professionally Same. At some scientists consists this equality already at the start of their career and can be achieved via the Career progression can be maintained. Other scientists on the other hand, partially reorganize themselves in the course of their careers, in particular re because she after the promotion only outside of the Science fixed Place or find part-time employment opportunities. Still others will only Career progression to professional peers by sharing their professionally advanced a partner in terms of professional status, professional responsibility and come catch up. Since it is not clear until late whether the professional goal of knowledge through a permanent position as a professor (or scientific che Councilor) can be made permanent, throw the professional insecurities for all couples have an increased need for planning. This draft of the future is made by Couple to couple configured differently, and the partners get in the Roles of the professional role model, the colleague, the provider of the seed children or the family breadwinner each have very different Interpretations for the professional development of female scientists. If Scientists in their partner a reliable force in the family area and an intellectual exchange at professional level. den, they can meet the demands of a science career at a in a way that enables compatibility with family. a couple dyna- mik, which is oriented towards overarching common goals, is with the

Realizing your own career is very helpful. The support of the ner can take different forms and also refer to the limit professional level. As mentors and strategic advisors, partners who support the scientist in her professional advancement Zen and for example their careers as a self-employed person to back up.

To what extent lack practical Support through the partner also in the case from science careers from Women *without* Children one role plays remains uncertain against the background of our evaluations, since this does not apply to any of the analyzed cases. scientists with children, who have no support in the private or professional area all the more dependent on the institutional framework. Find they have conditions in the science system that give them secure prospects and offer the possibility of flexible working, an ideal company Supporting partners in securing their own professional success. If you don't find them, your own career in the science system becomes a tightrope act.

In conclusion, it can be stated that in science predetermined institutional occasions, the until to the professorship no provide for permanent employment in one place, depending on the social structure tural and biographical origin of the scientists and depending ability from the respective dynamics in the Pair very differing to the layout the own career paths used become can. The case writings show that a purely educated middle-class background ground given familiarity with the scientific working method no necessary Pre-condition for the successful realization one represents a scientific career. The analysis also makes it clear which ambivalences in particular educational climbers in the present gene science system to be professionally successful and personally satisfactorily pursuing an academic career.

Scientific careers, as we have shown, make high demands ments to his candidacy. On the one hand, the ethos of scientific scientific profession as a vocation stubborn; it works deep into the life design of many scientists. Simultaneously are increasing in addition to the requirement of an academic appointment Dynamics of self-entrepreneurship required. [6] In the course of the waking send claim to the employability and appointment ability of scientists demands made by scientists on the skills of self-validation, Knowledge and contact maintenance as well as strategic skills in handicrafts the own Career go with one decoupling from effort andResult, i.e. H. scientific Success along and prompted Knowledge- scientific researchers to talk about scientific careers as "made to speak" (cf. Enders 2003).

Against the background of the special career conditions in science we have examined how women find their way into the scientific embark on a career and what motivates them on this path to a professorship to pursue. Women, the one science career strive, knowledge around the special requirements and act accordingly; but collide- combine their career orientations with other goals in life; a compatibility of work, partnership and family is due to a change of location, long working times and temporal restrictions one stepped at the age adapted qualification phase difficult to achieve. The science system tem offers (still) few possibilities for a joint change of location and no possibilities of an age-independent, individualized qualification phase or promising part-time management positions. for one Coping with the different tasks of a scientific employment requirement it currently Partner, the the Plan the Women support. Successful scientific careers are particularly Women denied, whose vocation in of their couple relationship lived becomes. In these couple relationships, the scientific careers of women are (with) designed, at the same time these couples reach the limits of their strength. organizational Toric demands of changing work locations and long working hours are experienced as unreasonable demands in the long run. Women, in turn, who are not in strong egalitarian oriented couple relationships integrated are, carry the Structuring of work and family primarily responsible alone. you are up institutional "niches" reliant or life without partnership (and

---

6 The concept of self-entrepreneur is related to the concept of science entrepreneur differentiate. the latter designated scientist and female scientists the itself professionally establish themselves at the interface of science and business as in the tech nik- and natural sciences to observe (Knee/Simon 2009: 537).

family) in the traditional sense of a common place of residence and mine spent free time.

The professional success of female scientists is thus present closely linked to the presence of supporting partners and not through institutional regulations secured by science. The sub Support for partners can take many forms and vary depending from the life plans of the couples to the professional area or focus on private life. For the professional success of knowledge However, it is currently the case that those who are particularly successful whose partners with them "together To have a career".

4.5 Attachment: short descriptions the cases

4.5.1 professional history and social structure case 1

At 40, Ms. Behrendt is slightly older than her partner. She is a social senschaftler and has her doctorate and habilitation in this subject completed. At the time of the survey, Ms. Behrendt was working as a professor sorin. Your partner is a doctor of natural sciences who is interviewed time at one research institute at his habilitation is working. The Couple has dual careers. The couple relationship between woman and man Behrendt began shortly after Ms. Behrendt and has existed for about 15 years. The couple has two children who are under ten year old are.

Since obtaining their university degrees, both partners have unapologetically scientific worked. Also were both almost continuously on changing temporary Place occupied, with the Exception the Maternity leave of less than half a year by Mrs. Behrendt and one each very short phase of unemployment of both partners to different time points. While Ms. Behrendt was doing her research at a graduate school scientific career starts, Mr. Behrendt works continuously Third-party funded or basic-funded full-time positions. Since my doctorate both partners to positions that were known through a longer contract are signed (more than five years). Ms. Behrendt describes her positions as such, on those she relative independent and free research could and at the same time a lot of positive support through the institutional embedding of their activity and by their superiors as well as sponsors ten has. Ms. and Mr. live and work until the birth of the first child Behrendt in different places for many years. For the birth of the first Child, they determine a common place of residence, which is based on the place of work from Mr Behrendt falls and at to the the common Children life. Woman Behrendt commutes for many years and until she takes up her professorship to their place of work. After that, the couple misplaced the common one primary residence at their place of work; now her partner commutes. Mrs. Behrendt has an educational background. Both parents were employed and employed in leadership positions in science. In the family from Mr Behrendt has the Father one academic Training and is employed, the Mother was in the first ten years of life the Children not working.

4.5.2 *professional history and social structure case 2*

Ms. Zeiher is almost 40 years old and nine years younger than her partner. She got her university degree in natural sciences, doctorate fourth and habilitation. At the time of the survey, Ms. Zeiher and her Partner both as professors in the same subject. They got to know each other in Ms. Zeiher's doctoral phase, when both were at the same scientific institute and Mr. Zeiher has just completed his habilitation. The couple relationship consists since more than ten years.

Without exception, Ms. Zeiher worked in science. she begins your career path in european Abroad, where she grew up and earned her university degree. Almost two years after graduation Finally, she moves to Germany, initially as a researcher colleague to work and then a PhD studies record. After Diploma of their promotion is working she seamless on changing, Temporary postdoc positions at various locations. On this She can research relatively independently. She achieves this by submits its own project proposals and selects the main topics that they interested. It is always well embedded institutionally. She has a big ßes professional network and receives a lot of support, especially at the beginning her career through her doctoral supervisor. Also the partner of Ms Zei- her has been working as a scientist without interruption since graduating. Until his habilitation, he finances himself primarily through scholarships. In the first half of the relationship, Mr. and Mrs. mainly in separate places. Ms. Zeiher commutes between the own location and that of your partner. Lives during her habilitation andthe couple works in the same city. With her appointment, Ms. Zeiher a professorship at a university more than five hundred kilometers away. Mr. and Mrs. Zeiher spend two to three weekends every month together. Neither Ms.

Zeiher's parents nor those of your husband have academic degrees acquired. While the Parents from Woman Zeiher both worked full-time without managerial positions, work only the father worked full-time in Mr. Zeiher's family Leading position.

4.5.3 *professional history and social structure case 3*

Woman Lehnert is How her partner something above 40 Years old. Your study degree in the natural sciences, in which she also movieed. At the time of the interview, she was working as a research assistant worker at a university. Your partner is also a scientist, who is employed as a research assistant at the time of the interview and at his habilitation is working. The Pair has one dual career. Woman and Mr. Lehnert got together at the end of their studies, which they did almost at the same time complete, met. At the time of the interview, the couple relationship hung for about fifteen years. They are married and have two Children under ten years old are.

Ms. Lehnert is looking for the same place as her pro-movierender partner first one appropriate Job and PhD with a scholarship. Unlike her partner, Ms. Lehnert turns to the promotion from the science off and is looking for a job in the scientific business-related area. She takes on a position that is interesting in terms of content not quite of their qualification is equivalent to, but after some Time indefinitely becomes. After the birth of the children, Ms. Lehnert loses vance of their employer this employment. Then she goes over two years of parental leave and makes another turn towards science science. She successfully applied for a postdoc grant that her enables scientific re-entry, and works as a scientific Scientific employee in changing research projects. the contractual lengths of academic activities are both before and after promotion rather short (under three years). In the contrast in addition is Mister Lehnert

–   with the exception of a short phase of unemployment directly after degree – continuously in science without changing careers busy. After Diploma the dissertation takes he one Job in the Abroad and commutes to their common place of residence. When the couple expects a child he returns back to the common place of residence. Mr. Lehnert works as scientific Employees and begins his habilitation. While in of Mr. Lehnert's family, neither parent has an academic degree in Ms. Lehnert's family, the father has an academic degree. The division of labor between Ms. Lehnert's parents was characterized by a traditional division of labor and unemployment of the mother. Also the courage ter of Mr. Lehnert was solely responsible for the care of the children, was at the same time she however full-time employed.

4.5.4 *professional history and social structure case 4*

Woman Thiel is meager 40 Years old and nine Years younger as her Partner. She has within the technical sciences her university degree and her PhD acquired. Her position as an academic councilor, which she view point in time and at which she habilitates, has recently been indefinitely been. Your partner is also a technical scientist with a doctorate for the interview time one employment in one private sector company has. Ms. and Mr. Thiel met a few years after study graduation from Woman Thiel met. To this time has Mr. Thiel already holds a doctorate. At the time of the interview, the couple drawing for about ten years. The couple is married and has one child, the under ten years old is.

After completing her studies, Ms. Thiel initially worked for a few nate at a large company in the private sector. After that changes she goes to the university and works as a research assistant. That is are their positions in science before and after their doctorate limited, but their employment contracts are of comparatively long duration. Already hers first occupation in the science goes over five years, and her postdoc position stabilizes before the completion of her habilitation. She also receives support from her doctoral supervisor after her doctorate. During the two-year parental leave, her employer allows her to can continue to work scientifically and "stay on the ball". In comparison to the uninterrupted professional career of Ms. Thiel, the professional run of the partner more versatile. After a short period of unemployment he begins his professional career with postgraduate studies, after which Graduated from a position as a research assistant. This falls into the period before the beginning of the relationship with Ms. Thiel. After one again, almost a year of unemployment, he switches to the private sector and has since worked for various companies. The first years of the relationship both live and work on two different things locations. During this time, Mr. Thiel commutes to his office several times a month partner. Even before Ms. Thiel became pregnant, her partner changed the employer and moves to the same city. Mrs. Thiel's parents have no higher education. Both were continuously employed; the mother first in part time, later also in full time and with management tasks.In Mr. Thiel's family, he worked continuously without managerial working father an academic degree. The mother worked until for the twelfth year of Mr. Thiel not.

5. Consequences of different interdependence arrangements for individual and dual careers

5.1 *Introduction: The Career Myth*

As explained in the second chapter of this book, scientists and scientists in academic partnerships gender specific Opportunities for double earner and single or single earner arrangements. The question in this chapter is to what extent such interdependence ter on the one hand your own career opportunities and on the other hand the chances for influence the realization of dual careers. So it's about the question ge, to what extent beyond a "mere" participation in working life knowledge workers and her Partners in the Position were, professional positions to achieve that corresponded to the educational investments made and perspective on professional (further) development (cf. Chapter 1 in this A book). Are scientists professionally successful? cher (ie they are more likely to have a career) if only they are in the partnership one employment pursue? And close temporary Alone- or. single earner arrangements inevitably later dual careers out of? At the answer this Questions should simultaneously in the literature common Explanations for the realization or failure of dual careers on the test bench be asked.

As a myth and at the same time as an institutional reality, career ensure a consistent and long-term connection to the labor market need – coupled with the opportunity to get through the support one more person on the "household front" completely his own to be able to devote to one's profession and professional development (cf. Beck-Gerns-home 1983; Genen 1994; Moen/Roehling 2005):

"(...) the career mystique requires two conditions: (1) an expanding economy with upward or at least secure occupational paths, and (2) workers with someone else – a full-time homemaker – to provide backup on the domestic front. Today, these two conditions are seldom met for either men or women." (Moen/Roehling 2005: 9)

If this is assumed for all highly qualified occupations, it can be assumed that that the Need, itself this myth to adapt in professional fields with long and more uncertain careers like science stronger available is. Because of the overwhelmingly temporary employment relationships below the professorship and the relatively limited professional alternatives after many years of employment in the science system the pressure on scientists increases, on the one hand spatially flexible to use existing options and, on the other hand, to be flexible in terms of time and with high working time intensity various indicators of success (such as publications ments third-party funding, project management, teaching experience) to serve, around this career requirements just to become or. the

"Myth of thoroughbred and full-time scientist" to maintain (Construction 2003: 243). Then succeed the vocation on one professorship and staying in academia is not, the scientists are due to the long qualification phases, as a rule too old to steiger/innen (with professional experience exclusively in research and teaching) to find a job outside of the scientific community (Room/Krimmer/stableman 2007: 104).

According to this career myth, those scientists and scientists better career opportunities have, the one years connection at the labour market show can and whose professional Development and operational readiness through one non-employment the partners was "supported". Scientists in single-earner arrangements should therefore have advantages over their colleagues in double have earning arrangements. [1]

In contrast, the career of scientist and scientists in single-earner partnerships,

ie in interweaving arrangements, in those she self longing phases the non-employment had, particularly endangered be. This assumptions are fed by the observation that careers in science society are (still) shaped by expectations that very often ideal type one "male normal biography" recourse (see. geen 1994; Moen 2010) (cf. chapter 1 in this book), i.e. to a vocational balanced lifestyle with a straightforward, seamless professional biography. The question of this chapter is to what extent these assumptions can be confirmed as well as why and when (under what conditions) dual careers den- still possible are.

---

1 In this chapter, long-standing interdependence term of the employment history of scientists and their partners those only the scientist or. the scientist employed is (see. Section

5.3 as well as Chapter 2 in this A book).

Consequences of different interdependence arrangements

5.2   *dual careers – the career myth for the Despite*

In dual career couples have - according to the career myth and the assumed "male normal biography" - actually both partners only limited opportunities to meet the above career requirements are equivalent to. nevertheless have she it done, that both partner not are "only" employed (in the sense of double earner couples), but also Career advancement appropriate to age and qualifications, in some cases up to leadership or top positions in your respective professions, reached have. How did these couples manage despite additional challenges? by coordinating two careers and despite the lack of support by a housewife/househusband not just one (or none at all), but to realize two careers? Why can't everyone do this? Couples who want this?

There are various explanations for this in the literature, which different possibilities of the couples due to their couple constellations (i.e. the combination of individual characteristics of the two partners), (non-) Emphasize responsibility for children and housing arrangements. The view on the *pair constellations* is in view of the career myth, among other things interesting because even couples with two wage earners feel compelled to do so could give priority to professional development (see Chapter tel 4 in this book) so that one of the two partners has a career at all can realize. Existing research findings actually indicate that that self in dual earner couples because of from mobility and or Availability requirements of the two professional activities as well as by the starting a family frequently the professional Development of a partner – often the man – who is given priority (cf. e.g. Ackers 2004; Bathmann/Müller/Cornelissen 2011; Becker/Moen 1999; Boyle etc al. 2001).

Nevertheless, there are also findings in the literature for other partner academic career strategies. On the one hand, there is a more "individualistic" sche" strategy, with which both partners relatively independently of each other their Pursue careers and both to correspond to the (male) career myth try (e.g. Bathmann/Müller/Cornelißen 2011; Dettmer/Hoff 2005; Millet/Herma/Schneider 2005).

On the other hand, couples also pursue an "egalitarian" or collective family strategy in which both partners are willing to work togetherlive cutbacks and compromises in relation to their own career take. With this arrangement, there may be restrictions on both re come, because the career potential in favor of the Family not be exhausted. Also responsible for this are certainly the many diverse "anti-partnership" requirements of professional careers (or the career myth) as well as the institutional *doing gender* – ie the unequal expectations and reactions on the professional and family commitment mind from men and Women (see. Bathmann/Müller/Cornelissen 2011; Becker/Moen 1999; Behnke/Meuser 2005; Millet/Herma/Schneider 2005).

On the one hand, the pursuit of different strategies is justified the gender, relationship and parenting concepts (cf. Bathmann/Mül- ler/Cornelißen 2011) as well as the career concepts of the couples or both partner (see. Chapter 3 and 4 in this book). On the other hand influencealso the balance of power between the partners, the gestures in the Pair and with it the realization conditions from careers (cf. Blood/Wolfe 1960).

The literature to household economics justified employment decision formation processes in pairs (cf. Becker 1991; Ott 2001) suggests *that differences in income* significantly reduce the chance of dual earners and Influencing dual career arrangements. Their realization is above all endangered if the partners earn different amounts. given the profits that can be made from a better-paying job, be it – so the argument goes – in the interest of both partners, this profit situation to maximize, creating either gainful employment favor the other in the pair is abandoned (e.g. when moving or when birth of children) or even if two persons are employed the requirements and professional development of the better serving partner is given priority. To a similar conclusion struggle come also exchange theoretical models – going back on Blood and Wolfe (1960): Those in the partnership have more resources has, thereby has a greater assertiveness for their own professional Interests (see. emerson 1976; Hood 1983). consequently can the expectation to be formulated that double careers with a higher Probability of "equal earning" couples (i.e. both partners have a similar Income) as from couples with income divorced realized can become.

In these theoretical approaches, the maximization of utility or the resource-based negotiation processes gender neutral conceptual ted. That is, regardless of gender, the partner or partner should better able to carry out his/her professional lien Interests enforce – under circumstances also on Costs the different careers and consequently a dual career. A series of serves, however, that a better negotiating position of the partner not to the same extent a waiver or limitation of professional development of the partner (cf. Bielby/Bielby 1992; Jürges 2006; Shauman 2010). Taking this into account, for the income relation tion in partnerships, a second expectation is formulated: double career are before everything in couples endangered, at those the Man (Knowledge-

schaftler or Partner) more earned, while she at one same or even higher incomes of the woman are more enforceable.

In a similar way, the *age constellation* in the partner schaft – and the (at least potentially) associated career gap if partners are not of the same age - for the realization of dual careers play a role. That is, in partnerships where the partners are different ages, the older partner could have a career advantage have. It is empirical and normative - even for highly qualified couples - usually the man is older than the woman (cf. Rusconi/Solga 2007; Solga/Rusco- ni/Krueger 2005). [2] The argumentation for the Connection from income human differences and career arrangements in partnerships following, could the older partner (or. if available, the older partner) better in the Position be, the own professional Interests in the partnership enforce. But also for the age constellation, earlier studies show investigations that they do not represent a purely temporal, gender-neutral relationship (cf. Rusconi/Solga 2007; Solga/Rusconi/Krüger 2005). Rather is to proceed from gender-coded concepts of age, so that it is from Meaning is, who – Man or Woman – older is. And so show alreadythe analyzes in the second chapter of this book that dual earner arrangements gements somewhat more frequently by couples with an atypical age constellation can be realized, ie by couples in which women (scientists women or partners) are older than their husbands. In this chapter should be examined to what extent they use their age advantage for the real from dual careers to use can. Because of from tuning Difficulties in aligning the (similar) career requirements ments, the expectation can also be formulated that people of the same age Partners are less likely to have dual careers in general to and in the Science in the special have as couples with one Age difference. The underlying question is: To what extent is an age-related equalization of the professional requirements for double careers, and this is particularly the case when both partner one scientific career realize want?

It is also known that the transition from a partnership to a Family (with children) professional development of women and men influenced differently (see Chapter 3 in this book). This is due to one of the social expectations and role attributions that by the women (internalized or due to a lack of external support options) lead to taking over the main responsibility for the *children* so that some women interrupt their professional commitments or to reduce (must). Other women don't wear anyway

---

2 It was also found in our study population that male scientists are older as her partners were, scientists but younger as her partner (see. Kapi phone 1 in this A book).

actually have the main responsibility and thus have a "double burden" - either due to a non-egalitarian claim on the partner society or because they have difficulties, also their egalitarian claim around- or push through to can (see. Chapter 3 in this A book; Hess/Rusconi 2010). This double burden can to one Disadvantage for her lead professional development. Second, women in general can and mothers in particular regardless of the actual organization and responsibility for child care through processes of statistical Discrimination (cf. e.g. England 2005) by their employers in their professional development are hampered, if not hindered. This is This is the case, for example, when male colleagues or childless colleagues solely on the basis of quantitative, but not qualitative, performance characteristics of promotions or the allocation of management tasks against be preferred over mothers. This could lead to double servant couples with children because of the potential restrictions the Career the Woman (Scientist or partner) fewer in the Position are to realize a dual career. That will be examined below be.

In addition, there is some evidence that work and family life are are particularly difficult to reconcile with science (cf. Lind 2008; Metz-Göckel/Selent/Schuermann 2010). For example, female scientists for example due to insecure job prospects and employment nit more often no Children as college graduates in general (Metz Göckel/Selent/Schuermann 2010: 19). On the one hand, the fear of disadvantages in their careers, many female scientists cancel or postpone it (cf. Lind 2008). On the other hand feel before mainly mothers, but increasingly also fathers in their professional development disadvantaged by colleagues and superiors (cf. Lind 2008). To the- after could be expected that couples where both partners in the Science employed are, less common dual careers with children realize can as occupationally heterogeneous couples. On the other hand, earlier analyzes s that couples with heterogeneous occupational backgrounds work in academia conceived as the one that can be better combined with childcare is - and with this justification, the task was then mostly the scientists to (see. Hess/Rusconi 2010; Hess/Rusconi/Solga 2011a). such gender stereotypes attributions from Working hours-or flexibility of work location are less possible in academic couples because here both partners practice the (allegedly) more flexible profession. consequently could alternatively be expected that careers of mothers and Speaking of which, dual careers with children are more likely to be in academically homogeneous in occupationally heterogeneous couples realized can become.

Finally, an academic career or probation as scientific offspring frequently the way of life one flexible and mobile singles (cf. Metz-Göckel/Selent/Schürmann 2010) or a single earning patterns of couples (cf. Geenen 1994). Especially for academic Geographical

mobility is an important factor for mixedly educated people part of professional careers, so that academics move on average often (cf. Becker et al. 2011; Büchel/Frick/Wit- te 2002; cutter etc al. 2008). This requires from high qualified couples
– who want to realize dual careers – often that they can use multi-local ler housing arrangements with this mobility requirements Step hold and thus a kind of "doubling of the 'male' career model" accomplish (Bathmann/Müller/Cornelissen 2011: 131f.). To that extent ver- It is not surprising that academic couples more frequently (than other educational groups) pen) live in multi-local living arrangements that are deprived of daily commuting, Weekend commutes to living-apart-together arrangements (LAT) enough (cf. Schneider et al. 2008). These living arrangements serve to to maintain or enable the professional career of both partners (cf. Schneider/Limmer/Ruckdeschel 2002). In addition, arise increased spatial mobility and the resulting multi-localquality of coexistence also out of the professional uncertainty because of of fixed-term contracts (cf. Becker et al. 2011; Schneider et al. 2008).

Even if multi-local housing arrangements allow for the realization of double can support pet careers, they are often associated with considerable time, financial and emotional costs (cf. Rhodes 2002; Schnei-der/Limmer/Ruckdeschel 2002). In addition, every career change can be linked to geographic mobility, so that there is a high level of flexibility in the Housing arrangements by the couples is required. Are not couples now willing to live in separate residences (LAT or long-distance commuting) may This leads to limitations in professional opportunities for one or both lead partners (cf. Jürges 1998a, b). A large number of studies show contribute to the fact that women are more likely to have their places of residence and work at the mobility Align the man's demands rather than the other way around - be it as "moving along" Partner (tied mover) or local property (tied stayer) (cf. Bielby/Bielby 1992; book 2000; Büchel/Frick/Witte 2002). [3]

Due to the predominantly temporary employment relationships, half of the professorship in the German university or science system as well such as the (discipline-specific) different spread of longer ones Stays abroad (e.g. as postdocs; cf. Hess/Rusconi/Solga 2011a; Zimmer/Krimmer/Stallmann 2007) as component one science run

---

[3] If this also applies to academically educated women and couples in general, one could Study on female natural scientists and engineers with doctorates (with activities within half and outside of science), however, show that none of these women after the Promotion corresponded to the type "tied stayer" or "tied mover" (Becker et al. 2011: 49f.). A common domicile with their partners has been among a large number of these women through longing daily commute times allows or. maintain.

bahn, it is to be expected that multi-local living arrangements - such as long-distance commute (i.e. more than daily commute to the workplace of one or even in the Partner) or LAT arrangements (ie separate Place of residence) – in academically homogeneous partnerships are more often the reality of couples than in occupational field heterogeneous couples. In addition could at science couples "immobile" living arrangements, ie living in a common Place without commuting or with maximum daily commuting, with larger ones Disadvantages for dual careers than for heterogeneous occupational fields couples.

Furthermore, it can be assumed that the partners in

scientific couples have to change their place of work more frequently than those who work outside of science. This can lead to a higher dynamic of housing arrangements lead to the former. Regarding the influence of different mobility dynamics can opposite expectations formulated become:

(a) Mobility dynamics that do not infra- or even allow the combination (i.e. an improvement) chen, carry dual careers. (b) professional Mobility, the with one change or deterioration of the living arrangement is connected, can the Danger increase that a career is put at disposal, and thereby also reduce the chance for a dual career.

These different hypotheses on the influence of pair constellations ments and interdependence arrangements on the career success of women and the realization from dual careers become in the following examined. To this end, it is first descriptively presented to what extent female scientists and scientists were able to accomplish a career and whether this is realized within the framework of single or double career arrangements became. In a second step, the importance of long-term interdependencies relationship patterns in partnerships. Here the career myth put to the test, and there will be answers to both initially formulated questions: To what extent are scientists senschaftler professionally more successful if only you in your partnership employment pursue? And in what way limit temporary Alone- or single-earner arrangements later dual career opportunities? in one third step, the hypotheses on the meaning of pair constellations lations regarding Income, Age, To be available from children andliving arrangement checked.

5.3 *Methods*

database this chapter are the standardized life course inter views the scientists as well as (separated) of their Partners. With it only those scientists are included in the analysis for whom a Interview of the partner is available (cf. chapter 1 in this book). there in This chapter focuses on the consequences of the entanglement arrangements in Couple and the influence of couple constellations for the realization of individual and dual careers, only those science are taken into account who have completed at least the last year of the observation period (see below) with this partner were. 4

As observation period for the interweaving pattern became the Life phase six to twelve years after the first degree scientist. The selection of this time span allows, the professional careers of the younger partners (and rarely younger partners) of the scientists who due to their age, later than the scientists received their first degree degree (cf. Section 5.4). Along the ones used here career definition and empirically at the majority the questioned Knowledge-schaftler/innen are the first six years after the Promotion as well as around the period in which the majority of respondents her first child (see Table 1.2 in Chapter 1 of this book). So it is a very critical phase in which most scientists (must) prepare for the transition to a professorship and in the professional and family demands can collide strongly. Since very few researchers who have not (yet) obtained their doctorate have been observed for so long they were generally (to avoid selection effects) from the sequence analysis excluded. The multivariate analyses for individual and Dual careers (at the time twelve years after graduation) therefore also only refer to those who had a doctorate at the time of the interview scientists and professors.

As discussed in more detail in the first chapter of this book, the partial participation in working life is not a sufficient characteristic for the presence a career; the decisive factors are the content of the activity and the prospect on one professional (further) development.

For scientists and Partners became based the information out of your interviews the Achieving a career as a professional position within or outside of science operationalized that matches its qualifications and institutional functional Old corresponded. [5] Based on it became dual careers as

---

4   10% of the scientists with a doctorate (incl. professors) were removed from the analysis se excluded because they were still single or with another partner at the time. ner together were.

5   For academic careers, twelve years after graduation are considered essential recriteria the exercise of highly qualified activities or the position as a scientific employee (incl. scholarships), the doctorate and the assumption of responsibility to to name (please refer Chapter 1 in this A book).

such employment constellations are defined in which both partners gene time a – in the senses just mentioned – had a career.

Based on the information provided by the scientists and their partners on their activities, the respective interdependence Arrangements of employment histories in the partnerships reconstructed (for one Description the applied Sequence- and cluster method see. Chapter 2 in this A book). The analysis the interweaving pattern the Employment histories in partnerships showed for the period six to twelve Years after study graduation next to the four already known inspect (sole and single earner as well as academically homogeneous and occupational terogenic dual earner arrangements; see Chapter 2 in this book) two other patterns that cannot be discussed in detail here. [6] How already discussed in detail in the second chapter of this book, it also shows for this period that female scientists significantly more frequently than theirs male Colleagues in scientifically homogeneous partnerships lived (29% vs. 12%), ie both partners were active in the scientific field. [7] Also, single-earner arrangements were due to a long-standing gene non-employment more often at scientists to find (14.5% vs. 1% of scientists). [8th] On the other hand, they took over substantially the sole breadwinner role less often than their male colleagues (5% vs. 32%). There are hardly any gender differences in the spread of occupational Field-heterogeneous double-income partnerships, i.e. couples in which the Scientists within and their partners outside of science shaft employed were (27% the scientists and 30% the Knowledge-schaftler).

For the analysis of the influence of the pair constellations on the chance Twelve years after graduation, the respective constellations one year before. The *income differences* in the couple were grouped into three categories: "Equally different Servant couples are those in which both partners earn about the same ten, while in the category "scientist more" the partners something fewer until significant fewer as the scientists earn

---

[6] On the one hand, this includes a small group of scientists (3%) who of this period was with the current

partner, but in the six years previously lived mostly as single or had a partner who was not the current partner is. On the other hand, there was a much larger group (21%) whose observation period shorter as the six Years was (in the median 31 Months).

7 quantitative descriptions became regarding of gender, the career level and Disciplines are weighted so that - as provided for in the sampling plan (cf. Chapter 1 in this A book) – always to same shares represent are.

Female scientists in single-earner partnerships were in the observation period in median 45 Months not employed, i.e. H. while meager three Quarter the Time ten, and vice versa in the "Partner more" category. 9 In the *age tellation* distinguish between two categories who in the partnership – knowledge employee or partner – is older. Couples where the age difference between the partners maximum twelve Months fraud, became as "even old" coded. The *presence of children* refers to the birth of the first biological child. Eventually, the *living arrangements were divided* into four Categories sho.wn:

- "In the same place" if the couple lived in the same place and a or both partners commuted to work daily at most (ie only during the day over at one other place of work were);
- "Fern commuting (ZP)" if the couple lived in the same place, but the Scientist for the removed Workplace commuted and there for stayed for several days/nights;
- "Long-distance commuting (PA)" if the couple lived in the same place but the Partners, each with a stay of several days, commuted while the Scientist at Residence remained
- "LAT", ie living-apart-together arrangements, if the partners separate residences lived and worked.

Before the importance of entanglement arrangements and pair constellations ments for realizing your own career and dual careers checked using multivariate analyzes (for details see Section 5.5), the next section describes how scientists scientists were able to start their own careers working and how this in the frame one Double career happened.

5.4   One or two careers?

Six Years after study graduation had the majority the scientist and female scientists a career according to the above career definition. This was slightly more common among men than among men Women (79% vs. 69%). scientist and scientists under- differed far more in which partnership constellation they realized their careers: It is true for both of them that a double career constellation the most common arrangement was (43% or. 51%; Illustration 5.1) – but while more than three quarters of female scientists with a career Part one dual career couple was, were it at the male Colleagues

---

8   The income and housing constellations were based on the information provided by the scientists on the income relation and the living arrangement in the partnership while of their to to the time exercised Task coded.

9

only about half (77% vs. 55%, not shown). In contrast to realized over a third of the scientists, but only 15% of their colleagues a career in a one-career arrangement. Furthermore realized at almost a quarter of female scientists, but just 10% of their colleagues only the partner creates a career. In sum, this means: If women in partnerships have a career, then usually "common sam" with the partner. For scientists, however, this is far less frequently the Case.

Another clear difference between scientists and scientists senschaftlerinnen consists in the reasons for a missing career. The male scientist without Career (six Years after degree ending) were overwhelmingly employed or scholarship holders (81%). The means they were employed, albeit not (according to the defined career definition) appropriate to education and age. For example, they had way still no Promotion. At the scientists without Career on the other hand, only just under half were employed (49%). your missing career left more often than their non-employed colleagues along. [10]

[10] A quarter of these scientists (but none of their non-career colleagues) were in maternity leave Another 10% of scientists without a career were unemployed; the theirs were pursuing another activity (e.g. further studies) (16% of the women and 8th% the Men without Career).

We see the same with our partners: almost three times as much many partner How partners without Career were employed (65% vs. 23%). One of the reasons for this was that twice as many female partners as Partner has not yet obtained an academic degree at this time (19% vs. 9%) - and therefore do not yet have/start a career could. The cause is, among other things, in the age-typical partner choice: the men were mostly older than their partners. The Partners who do not yet have an academic degree at this point in time were on average 5.5 years younger than their partners. As with the science However, it can also be observed among the partners that a lack of career among women more frequently than among men with a non- employment connected is. [11]

Even twelve years after the first degree, most of the ing majority of scientists have a career (86% and 73% respectively). Once again it is evident that female scientists are pursuing their careers realized mainly within the framework of a dual career arrangement: Bei almost three quarters of the female scientists with a career had their partner also have a career, while fewer than half of their peers have gene with career was the case (72% vs. 47%, not shown). Although science scientist and scientists to this time even something had a career themselves more often than six years previously, double Servant partnerships are no longer the most common for male scientists career constellation (40.5% vs. 53% of female scientists; tion 5.1). At this time, scientists now (if also scarce) the one-career constellation, in which only she herself has a career had (45%). At the scientists came this constellation only half so frequently before. one-career constellations, at those only the Part- ners had a career, for male scientists the exception, while they still agree with about 16% of their colleagues fen. This shows once again that scientific careers are predominantly made up of women enough as part of from dual careers take place and dual careers – inside and outside of science - mostly due to a lack of one Career of scientists or partners fail.

Unlike six years earlier, both the scientific men and women scientists without a career mostly employed, if also not educational and age appropriate (96% or. 72%). [12] So had she for example still no promotion or no managerial duties. At

---

[11] A quarter of the partners without a career (but no partner) was on parental leave. About 11% of the partners and 9% of the partners were unemployed, the others went to other activities ten after (23% the Women and 18% the Men).

[12] Another 15% of the scientists – and again no colleagues – were on parental leave. 11% of the scientists (and no colleague) were unemployed. The others complete ten a additional Studies.

the male partners without a career were also more than

three four- phone employed, at the partners however fewer as the half (77% vs. 40%). Now, however, the unfinished study was no longer dium the cause of it, but above all the parental leave. [13]

In summary, the following can be stated: scientists and scientists run in partnerships were on the one hand relatively successful, a career to achieve, ie to achieve a professional position that matches their qualifications cation and its institutional age. The vast majority of male and female scientists had twelve years after study service completion of a career. On the other hand, only about half of the senschaftler/innen successfully in this "together" with their partners to to realize. The Fail from dual careers was mostly due a lack of a career for women, be it due to non-employment (above all with the partners of the scientists) or because the job position was not education and age-appropriate (especially in the case of scientists).

However, careers are not made "overnight", they are The result of many years of professional development - which is also at the most men and women in a partnership takes place. What Interweaving arrangements of the career paths Scientists and their Partners practice was discussed in Section 5.3 and in more detail in Chapter tel 2 of this book. The following section will now examine become, which Influence this interweaving pattern on the realization of careers of scientists as well as of dual careers.

5.5 The career myth put to the test

The question of the extent to which interdependence patterns existed in the previous six years were practiced, the (time-defined) probability of a career and from dual careers influence, became using from linear probability regressions examined. [14] The pictured regression coefficients press

---

13 Because at that time only one partner did not have a partner Academic degree. About a quarter of the partners without a career were on parental leave (9% of men), another 10% were unemployed (6% of men), the others left one others activity (e.g. B. one further Studies or Internship) after.

14 Next to the interweaving patterns and the pair constellations check the models for other features that are not discussed in detail. With the scientists ments: graduation cohort, discipline of the first degree, birth in East or West Germany country, employment of mother during childhood, academic education of parents, Duration of the activity carried out at the time, promotion. For the partners: employment in the public sector or private sector, fixed-term employment ses, promotion as well as for the subject homogeneity in the Pair.

depending on the interdependence arrangement, increase the probability of knowledge 12 years after graduation to have a career or a dual career, which compares the different groups allowed.

As Figure 5.2 shows, dual earner arrangements did not have one negative influence on the probability of female scientists Scientists to have a career twelve years after graduation. Male scientists with (in the previous six years) scientific had homogeneous or occupationally heterogeneous dual earner arrangements are just as likely to have a career as their peers single earner arrangements. The is called, the employment or Not- employment of the partner had for the professional development of the male lien scientist neither Before- still Disadvantages. In the Difference in addition decreased the Alone- as well as the single earner arrangement at Knowledge- their career opportunities. The probability of a ne career was with the (few) female scientists who had taken on the role of servant, only half the size of their male counterparts Single-earner colleagues and, as with colleagues with dual-earner arrangements.

That non-employment for men and women (academic students and Partners) one can have different meanings or not to the same extent of support for professional development of the other partner by being responsible for "private matters". serves the "household front", is also used in the difference between learn and scientists with temporary single-earner arrangement ments clearly. The (very few) male scientists working in the had been unemployed for long periods six years earlier not only twice as high a career chance as their colleagues with the same arrangement, but also the highest career probability. This initially counterintuitive result is be explained by the fact that these scientists spent their time of non- employment,

for example for further studies or an internship ten and not - How frequently at her Colleagues – their work due to from unemployment or interrupted parental leave.

As an interim conclusion, it should be emphasized that dual earner arrangements for both men and women scientists compared to single-earner arrangements are no obstacle to the realization of their individual visual professional careers represent. This is applicable in addition for knowledge- shaft-homogeneous How occupational field heterogeneous dual earner arrangements. That is, scientists who are part of a scientific couple can realize their own career just as often as colleagues, whose Partners outside of of science area employed are. One accordance of professional field brings so neither Advantages for the own Career based on a "shared knowledge" and better opportunities of Support between partners (see. Hess/Rusconi/Solga 2011a) still Disadvantages due to increased competition or coordination difficulties ten of similar professional requirements. Furthermore, it shows - in particular - re for Men –, that temporary single earner arrangements, ie longer Phases of non-employment, not necessarily a career obstacle represent, namely not when they are in phases of further qualification represent. Since the temporary non-employment of female scientists However, more often than men with parental leave or unemployment was bound, the "brittle" professional biography often led them to that she is twelve years after Diploma not adequate occupied were.

If you now look from the individual to the dual career, however, a different picture emerges (Figure 5.2). On the one hand, double to a much lesser extent than individual careers. ted become. For the others are the differences within the both Gender groups with regard to the influence of the different braiding arrangements significantly less. For example, female scientists in long-term dual earner arrangements a very similar probability ability for double careers like their colleagues, who for longer phases not employed or (less common) the sole earners were. Positive considered, this means that - contrary to the formulation often found in the literature expectation - a delay or interruption of one's own business with female scientists who temporarily work in traditional single-income live in partnerships does not lead to any additional disadvantage. In negative However, this also means that the probability of the realization dual careers – regardless of the relationship within the partnership braiding arrangement – are relatively small and thus also the (often laborious) me) Accomplishment of long-term dual earner arrangements none guarantee for dual careers.

This lack of benefit of dual earner for dual career arrangements tion is more evident among male scientists and their partners run. For scientists, dual careers are partnerships almost improbable. The reasons for this are above above all career restrictions with their partners due to a not adequate employment (rarely due to non-employment). A lighter Advantage of realizing two careers in different ones occupational fields compared to academically homogeneous couples is also evident in the scientists.

Absolutely striking differences is there however between men and Women. scientists in scientifically homogeneous double Servant arrangements have three times the double-career probability like their male colleagues. A slightly smaller gender difference shows itself for occupational field heterogeneous dual earner couples, at those it also the scientists and your partners more often succeeded one dual career to realize as the scientists and their partners. A key explanation for this is that dual careers mostly fail because of the female career (see above) – but this among other things, due to random sampling, less frequently among female scientists than is the case with the partners. [15] Nevertheless, this also shows extremely "positive" selected group of people, that at more than twice so many scientists How scientists the dual career failed because she herself had no career (52% vs. 20%).

---

15 In order to be able to take part in the survey, they had to be at a university and at a of the four career levels (including the professorship), i.e. at least for the At the time of the survey, they were employed in the science system and some of them had by definition one "Career" (see. Chapter 1 in this A book).

5.6   The influence of the pair constellations on dual careers

The question now arises to what extent different pairs constellations the realization of dual careers for men and women influenced. Which of the expectations formulated in the second section can be confirmed and which not? To answer these questions too delivery, became (separated for scientist and scientists) also estimated linear probability regressions, which depending on the pair constellation lation the probability of scientists to express, one dual career twelve years after study graduation to have. [16]

5.6.1 Income differences: same Money = same Career?

Two expectations were set for the income constellation in partnerships gene formulated: For the a one budgetary economics – gender neutral
–   Assumption that dual careers are more likely to probability of "equal earning" couples than couples with income divorced realized become can. For the others under inclusion one gender-unequal usability of power resources in the couple, that differences in income only increase the probability of a double decrease if the man (scientist or partner) spends more serves, not however if the Woman (Scientist or partner) asame or even higher income.

For female scientists with double earnings from a heterogeneous occupational field arrangement appears itself the first assumption to confirm (Illustration5.3). Because double careers are much more common with the same income as at income inequalities in the Pair. Lies a income differed, it does not play a role in the probability of a dual career It doesn't matter whether the woman or the man earns more. In science-homogeneous dual earner couples play income gap however no Role for the likelihood of dual careers. A possible explanation tion for the different Influence the income constellation in homogeneous and heterogeneous Dual Earner Partnerships the Knowledge- Scientists provide the results of an earlier analysis of the data. In this could shown become (see. Hess/Rusconi/Solga 2011a), that at scientists in occupational field heterogeneous partnerships the Value of their scientific Work partially from the partners in question placed

---

16 Next to the interweaving patterns and the pair constellations check the models for further Characteristics, on the not closer received will (cf. footnote 14).

became. Due to long-term job insecurity and the extensive th so-called qualification phase (a term used for a person who unfamiliar with the science system may raise doubts could, to what extent it is a "real" job at all or rather is a kind of extended study) it could be for scientists difficult to enforce that their career claims and requests changes in professional field-heterogeneous partnerships are given equal to be sighted. As a result, a separate career and a double career be more feasible in these partnerships if at least the come similar high is. Because of one "shared Attitude" for the Profession (see. Hess/Rusconi/Solga 2011a) could in science couples the A-have no or only a subordinate role in negotiation processesplay.

Source: record "Together Career make"; own calculations; weighted Declarations   □

The situation is somewhat different for male scientists. Firstly, in professionally heterogeneous partnerships, there is the probability essential for dual careers for couples with an income difference much higher than for couples where both partners earn the same amount. The- This finding therefore contradicts the budgetary economic assumption. In addition gives it at the even much earning couples here none Difference between scientifically homogeneous and professionally heterogeneous couples. This lays suggesting that the value of men's work within or outside of the Science is not valued differently like this however at the scientists the case is (please refer above). To that extent gives there is no gender-neutral perception of the value of work. Much more is this dependent on the gender of the person doing the work, as well as of the relation to the respective occupation of the partner. Then due to horizontal occupational segregation, male and female lich partner the scientists in the different professions unequally distributed. [17]

Although the differences between male scientists in professional field heterogeneous partnerships are larger, the income relation even in the case of academically homogeneous intertwining arrangements Role. In the latter case, scientists had more than their partners earned, a higher dual career probability both in equal to their colleagues, who earned the same as their partners, when also to the (few) colleagues who earn less than their partners This finding also contradicts the second formulated expectation tion, because dual careers should be found less frequently in those couples at where the man deserves more.

In summary, both assumptions about the influence of income differences in partnerships are neither clearly refuted nor confirmed be taken. Equal income means –

especially in partners male scientists – not automatically an "equal safety" of career opportunities in the partnership, nor does a resource inequality inevitably double careers – not even if the man earns the higher income. The findings also show that the income relation before everything one role at occupational field heterogeneous couples plays, in which due to the different professions exercised, the emergency need for additional "mediation work" or explanation of the stay career requirements and -logics consists (see. Hess/Rusconi/ Solga 2011a). This shows that in occupational heterogeneous arrangements the scientists rather in the Position were, dual careers (and thus a career of their own) if they are as much as yours Partners earned, while partners were more likely to do so when their Income higher than that of the scientist was. This could be a hint ensure that the negotiations in partnerships about and the perception of the value of work is neither gender-neutral nor occupation-neutral are.

---

17 Of the employed (occupationally heterogeneous) partners at the time, the Partners of the scientists very often work as teachers (31% vs. 7% of the partners ner), while the male partners of female scientists are more likely to work in business company management, consulting and auditing (21.5% vs. 5% of the partners) or as an in- formatter (26% vs. 7%) and engineers (16% vs. 4%) were active.

5.6.2 *Age constellation: Goes the older before?*

Beyond income, the second section became expectation formulated that dual careers are more common in couples with atypical age constellation occur, i.e. in couples in which the women (scientific workers or Partners) older as her Men are. The same it was assumed that a synchronization of career requirements with equal partnerships lead to a lower probability of double ration – especially in of science - to lead can.

Figure 5.4 shows that female scientists in academic like and occupational field heterogeneous dual earner arrangements the Age constellation only plays a subordinate role. the probability honesty for dual careers is similar high in partnerships with or without age difference as well as independent of that, who – woman or man – the older one is in the partnership. For the question of whether after many gene single earner arrangements dual careers possible are, plays the Age constellation, on the other hand, plays an important role. Achieving a card re despite longtime interruption succeed with one clearly higher Probability of female scientists in partnerships of the same age ten. [18] The same applies to male scientists with many years of experience single earner arrangements. Here, too, double careers were years of non-employment of the partner with a higher probability probability in scientists with a peer or (typically) to find a younger partner.

The is called simultaneously, in peers partnerships consists on the one hand a higher risk for single-breadwinner arrangements (cf. Chapter 2 in this book), on the other hand, but also a greater chance of this at a later date Time to expand in careers for both partners. a possible The obvious explanation for this would be that not only, but above all, partners of the same age expect that two jobs will lead to contradictions and conflicts of the job demands of two careers. The- ser "Incompatibility" attempt she phased with one traditional division of labour and the concentration on only one (the male) Career to escape. There is then a head start for the male partner and his career "secured", the career of the partner can follow.

The greater difficulty of same-age couples, despite a long-standing dual earner arrangements one dual career to realize becomes particularly clear among male scientists (Figure 5.4). scientist with one peers partner had in particular in scientifically homogeneous, but also in occupational field heterogeneous couples one

---

18 Due to the insufficient number of cases for single-earner partnerships in which the knowledge partner was older than her partner, this atypical age constellation is not here received.

clearly lesser Dual Career Probability as her Colleagues in Partnerships in which the age difference for a partial equalization of professional requirements was helpful. The highest probability However, male scientists also had the potential for dual careers an atypical age constellation. This applies above all to scientific homogeneous couple relationships: scientist with one older partner were twice as likely to have dual careers as their peers laying with a (typical) younger partner. In fact, the "elder- ren" partners to have been better able to use their age advantage in own careers and through this in dual careers implement. possible There were often partners who, due to an age advantage, were in their careers already advanced were, fewer ready, this at difficulties to the disposition to place, as the Partners, at those the man was advanced in professional development. Or but Partners with an age advantage in the partnership had to come along expect fewer disadvantages when making professional compromises, since they already secured positions or even top positions (How one Professorship) reached had.

In summary, it can be seen that the very low dual career probability among male scientists in homosexual common double earner couples (cf. section 5.5) partly on the higher proportion of partnerships of the same age can be traced back – because this couples have larger Difficulties, time- and equal status two careers to be realized in science. In addition, for dual-income partners observable that an atypical age constellation in the did better Possibilities for dual careers offers.

5.6.3 *Children: dual careers only without Children)?*

Children should - so the expectation - even with double earner couples Restrictions in the career of women (scientist or partner rin) and thus lead to double careers. In addition, became theoretical reasonably expected that this (double) career risk both in scientific shaft-homogeneous as also in occupational field heterogeneous partnerships highis.

For scientists with occupational field heterogeneous dual earner constellation duration independent from the To be available from children one similarly high probability of a dual career (Figure 5.5). [19] The same only small differences gives it between scientistswith and without child(ren) in academically homogeneous double-earner couples. Here, the dual career probability for mothers was even slightly higher than childless female scientists. At the same time, this means that scientists with longstanding dual earner arrangements the Failure or the professional success of the two partners is not primarily dependent on the responsibility for children has been dependent.

The situation is different for female scientists with long-term single-earner arrangements. Here, childless scientists one 3 times so height Dual Career Probability like her colleagues with at least one biological child. A possible Explanation for this is that these (few) women who are without responsibility not doing any (paid) work for a child for a long time, this phase could use to gain further qualifications, so that their later better career opportunities reduced have.

In the synopsis of these findings, it is clear for scientists ensure that only in the case of long-term single-earner arrangements do the opportunities cen for one dual career with the birth from children reduce. Succeed

---

19 At this time, 64% of the scientists had at least one biological child (scientifically homogeneous couples 59%, occupationally heterogeneous 63%). scientists with before longstanding single earner arrangements were above average often mothers (83%).

Source: record "Together Career make"; own calculations; weighted Declarations

If you look at scientists with children, however, you see something different image. First, they less often realize two with their partners Academic careers with child(ren) than without. In contrast, play secondly, children in the realization of dual careers in occupational rogen double earner couples, i.e. if the partner is outside of senschaft is employed, does not matter. [20] scientists and their partners to with occupational field heterogeneous dual earner arrangement had one four times like that height probability with (or despite) child one dual career

---

[20] To this time had 56% the scientist at least a bodily Child. male scientist in scientifically homogeneous dual earner couples were childless slightly more often than their colleagues in heterogeneous professional relationships (52% vs. 37%).

to realize how their colleagues with scientifically homogeneous arrangements ment. In the case of the latter, double careers failed mainly due to the career other partners who are also scientifically active, but also to some extent in the career of scientists. That is, the birth of children leads te more often within the Science to one (at least temporary) Career break than in activities outside. Third, were - in difference to the scientists – the low Dual Career Opportunities at single earner arrangements (ie the partner was not employed) not due to the presence of children.

Given the primary responsibility of female partners in male chen scientists for child care and less frequent use from external facilities or care lines through Third (see. Chapter 3 in this book and Hess/Rusconi 2010) points out the difference between scientifically homogeneous and professionally heterogeneous partnerships of the male scientists pointed out that the time-consuming response for children worse with the spatio-temporal requirements from science careers is compatible as with careers outside of.

5.6.4 *Housing arrangements: Mobile and successful?*

given the high mobility requirements because of from temporary contracts as well as (differs depending on the discipline) stays abroad as part of the scientific career was expected on the one hand, that multi-local living arrangements are more common among academic couples spreads are. On the other hand, it was assumed that "immobile" housing arrangements ments, ie living in a common place without commuting or with daily commuting, with disadvantages for the realization of dual careers are connected - and this to a greater extent in the case of scientifically homogeneous ones as at occupational field heterogeneous double earner couples.

First of all, it should be noted that almost two thirds of the scientists lived in the same place as their partners, so that they or their partners employees did not have to commute to work at all or at most every day. Here- on the one hand, there are the differences between occupational field heterogeneous and scientifically homogeneous dual earner couples relative small amount (66% vs. 60%). Nevertheless, scientists lived in scientifically homogeneous communities Couples live in separate places almost twice as often as their colleagues in heterogeneous couples (22% vs. 13%), while the latter are more common long-distance commuting arrangements led. [21] For the others lived Scientist-

---

[21] The differences between academically homogeneous and professionally heterogeneous partners ties are more pronounced among male scientists than among female ones. About it Furthermore, in all dual-income partnerships, the men commuted more frequently (the

scientist or the Partner) as the women away.

to with A- or single earner arrangements more often in "real estate" housing arrangements (75% or. 70%). The concentration on only one employment or Career enabled therewith in higher Dimensions the Partners living together in the same place. dual earner arrangements required however more often – however not majority – multilocal housing arrangements.

Nevertheless, the question arises as to whether multi-local housing actually "reward" and if so, for which couples? Figure 5.6 shows that for female scientists multi-locality, especially in partnerships with heterogeneous occupational fields one higher dual career probability. the science scientists with occupational field heterogeneous LAT couple relationships had a higher dual career probability compared to their peers women who lived in the same place with their partner, but above all in right away with her colleagues in academically homogeneous partnerships LAT arrangements. [22]

---

[22] Because of to lower case numbers becomes on some long-distance commuting arrangements as well as on A-earner arrangements not closer received.

The fact that multi-local living arrangements for scientists with scientific homosexual couple relationships are not advantageous, does not mean, however, that they are disadvantageous. So are the differences between these female workers with mobile and immobile living arrangements relatively low. Included gives it only one Exception: female scientists the self for the long-distance commuting to work did not have a higher, but a significantly lower less likely to have a double career than their "immobile" colleagues. However, the latter also applies to couples with heterogeneous occupations. dual career ren failed here mainly because of the missing career of the partner. The Long-distance commuting of these female scientists was therefore not disadvantageous for them own career, but for the double career in Pair.

The findings for the male scientists also suggest that multilocality the chance for one own Career the partners and thus for a double career as a couple despite many years of non-employment ability of the partner can open up. Scientists with many years of sole Servant arrangements then had a significantly higher dual career perception probability if they lived in separate places. A comparative one also had a high probability of having a dual career ler with occupational field heterogeneous dual earner arrangements – however relatively independent of their living arrangements. As opposed to know- In professionally heterogeneous partnerships, homosexual couples will Life at the same Location not with lesser Dual Career Opportunities "be- punishes". [23] One possible Explanation therefor lies in to the from partners frequently practiced teaching profession (cf. Section 5.1), with which the living and working in one place seems to be more possible - and this, without being restricted in the adequate professional development be. [24]

in summary can man hold onto, that scientifically homogeneous Dual Earner Partnerships more often with multilocal types of housing accompanied as occupational field heterogeneous. Only for male scientist could the expectation be confirmed that "immobile" living arrangements with greater disadvantages for the realization of scientifically homogeneous tend to be associated with dual careers that are heterogeneous in the occupational field. to emphasize is also the outstanding positive Influence from multilocal housing arrangement

---

23 As with female scientists, the probability of dual careers in scientific homogeneous partnerships even lower for scientists who themselves work remotely delten. However, as with her colleagues, this did not diminish the chances for one of her own Career, rather for the Career the partner (and consequently for dual careers).

24 Despite the responsibility of the federal states for the teachers, what moves across state borders formally more complicated, a survey of German universities showed that University administrations then saw themselves in a position to support the partner's job search ment of newly appointed professors and thereby the life and work of the partners a common place if they worked as teachers (cf. Russia coni/Solga 2002; Solga/Rusconi 2004).

ments for the careers of partners with long periods of employment lack and consequently for the realization of dual careers as well in partnerships in which a gainful employment task was "waived".

However, living arrangements are – like any interweaving arrangement – dynamic and can change over time, with requirements and with change possibilities. Regarding the question of whether science couples one higher dynamics the housing arrangements subject as couples, at those the partners are active outside of science, it turned out that this only at male scientists the case is. Meager a Quarter the male scientist with a heterogeneous occupational field arrangement no change in living arrangements due to a change of employer the partner, while such stability only in a scientist could be found with a scientifically homogeneous arrangement. The differences between female scientists, on the other hand, were very low: on something more female scientists in academically homogeneous than in occupational rogens partnerships had the Partner no change of employer, the to changes in to the housing arrangement (17% vs. 11%).

In dual-income couples with heterogeneous occupations, it was particularly male scientists, but also among female scientists, the dual career probability higher if the partner does not have an employer there was a change that led to changes in the living arrangement (Fig. 5.7). Dual careers are therefore more likely to be achieved by those couples in which the professional activity of the partners no (additional) mobility adjustments brought with it. This finding suggests that partnerships and dual careers need a certain stability. Although that too If the difference is a little smaller, the same applies to males Scientists with single wage earners and for female scientists with single wage earners arrangements, ie in which the woman (partner or researcher) rin) has not been employed for a long time. In scientifically homogeneous double income earner couples, on the other hand, there was no difference between knowledge female workers whose partners have no or one or more "mobile" workers had a change of employer. This in turn means that this scientist to regarding the realization from dual careers fewer from the stability of their partners' place of residence than their female colleagues Partners with activities outside of science. Because with them it was

Risk higher that spatial stability (also) in their partners with career restrictions. That is, although an activity of the partner/ the partner in the Science not absolutely more often with mobile changing employers goes along so are but in the Science this change rather necessary, around educational and age appropriate positions to and thus also to combine (scientifically homogeneous) double careers real.

5.6   *Conclusion*

In this chapter the consequences of the interweaving patterns in the Employment history of partnerships for the realization of one's own (Science) career and examined for dual careers. Furthermore- out were the different options of the couples because of their couple constellations, Responsibility for Children and housing arrangements explored.

In general, it shows , *first* , that there are more scientists than Female scientists succeeded in finding professional positions appropriate to education and age (twelve years after graduation: 86% vs. 73%). Despite this However, high proportions of academics with careers were *second* dual careers no way the predominant partnership arrange ment; because only half of the scientists and two-fifths of the scientist realised one dual career in the Pair. Despite higher image

dung and labor participation in the Partners is the realization of dual careers in academic partnerships therefore no self-confidence steadfastness. *Thirdly,* dual careers mostly fail due to the "missing the woman's career. In almost every second partnership in science male scientists and every sixth female scientist able to achieve an education and age-appropriate professional position. This means that in these partnerships there was a prioritization of the career of the male partner instead. On the other hand, women in partnerships had one career, then in usually "together" with her Partner.

Not only are women less likely to achieve careers that are appropriate for their education and age, positions, they also had frequent (long) periods of non-employment task. In the period of six to twelve years after graduation almost every seventh female scientist practices a single-earner arrangement, mostly because of parental leave or unemployment was employed. In contrast, almost a third were their colleagues the sole breadwinner in the partnership. According to the career myth, should these male scientists thanks to their long-term connection to the labor market combined with the support of a non-employed ge partner who have the "best" career opportunities. Contrary to this myth show the findings of this chapter that such a gender-typical Division of labor in the couple is not "worth it" insofar as it affects career prospects of women (at best only in the short and medium term), but to no one advantage for the careers of male scientists. the career according to remythos, female scientists had to, but not their male colleagues, expect career disadvantages if they agree servant arrangements with longer interruptions of one's own professional ability practiced. The Difference between male and female scientists and between mothers and childless scientists run with single earner arrangements clarified however, that not every (Long-term) non-employment per se leads to a disadvantage, but especially when this is due to parental leave or unemployment done. If, on the other hand, this time is used for further qualification, then puts this arrangement not a career obstacle.

For dual careers, however, the picture is different: on the one hand, becoming Double careers realized much less frequently than individual careers, on the other the differences depending on the interweaving arrangement are significantly smaller eng. Especially female scientists in long-term double-income arrangements gements had a double carburization with a very similar probability like her colleagues who are not employed for long periods or who (rarely) who were the sole breadwinners. The same was true for males Scholars with sole and (less commonly) single earner arrangements compared to their colleagues in

dual-income workers with heterogeneous occupations partnerships. On the one hand closes so the gender typical (but also-atypical) long-term "renunciation" of gainful employment not necessarily fig later double careers, on the other hand the (often arduous) long-term gene accomplishment and coordination of two jobs none guarantee for dual careers. The is called, dual earner arrangements
do not "protect" against prioritizing professional development (to most of time the des male partner) (cf. Chapter 4 in this A book).

The Missing Advantage of Dual Earner Arrangements for Dual Car- ration is particularly clear in the case of academically homogeneous partnerships. The realization of two careers succeeds - especially for men scientists, but also among their female colleagues - much more rarely, if both partners pursue academic careers than if the partners ner outside of of professional field Science employed are. Despite long-years of employment, it is primarily the female partners (science collaborators or partners of scientists) who are not adequate were busy. The findings on the influence of the age constellation in the Partnerships of the male scientists suggest that a causal The reason for this lies in the greater difficulties of the couples, time and status to realize two scientific careers at the same time. An (age-related) development Distortion of the synchronization of (similar) professional requirements is after conducive to dual careers. In view of this, see each other above all same-age couples, at least temporarily with this incompatibility a traditional division of labor (see Chapter 2 in this book) or a Prioritizing the professional development of the male partner senior This strategy closes that is later dual careers not out of (How also the findings for female scientists with traditional single-income show arrangements), but it is undoubtedly quite risky and involves a (at best only temporary) disadvantage for well-qualified women and contributes to the (re-)production of inequalities in the world of work and in nerships.

The findings for male scientists also make it clear that Couples also have greater difficulty two science careers to realize when they are responsible for children. That this is not can be observed in female scientists lies, among other things, in their - much more frequent and earlier use of external care facilities and support services provided by third parties (vs. a main material support by the partners at the scientists; see. Chapter 3 in this book and Hess/Rusconi 2010; Hess/Rusconi/Solga 2011a). The is called, Children mean not by see a career break for women – not even in science – but it depends to a large extent on the respective care arrangements (see Chapter 3 in this book). However, the fact that male scientists in occupational Terogenic partnerships double careers with child(ren) are more possible as in science couples (there the partners with professions outside of the Science with less disadvantages for the own Career calculate had to), should encourage universities and scientific institutions to to seek life-phase-specific solutions, as well as the scientific system and its career requirements can be designed more flexibly (see. Hess/Rusconi/Solga 2011b).

Another hurdle to realizing dual careers – ahead especially in science - represent mobility requirements. Albeit science couples only partly more often as occupational field heterogeneous couples practice multi-local housing arrangements and adapt them to work sen (must) is such a "mobility" for careers in science rather necessary. Employer – and in great colleges and Knowledge- corporate facilities – can start with the establishment and expansion of Dual career services and with job offers for the partners contribute to the fact that "making a career together" is not synonymous trend with a long-standing, if not permanent, spatial separation the partner is; or that for a Living together on one appropriate professional development (if not employment) one of the partner is waived.

To actually dual career and not "only" dual earner couples to promote, dual-career offers should, on the one hand, already be for couples in earlier Career phases should be available (and not only from the professorship), on the other hand, be appropriate to the qualifications of the partners and offer a view of professional (further) development (cf. Hess/Rusconi/ Solga 2011b). Then How the findings this Chapter clearly show is even in the case of academic couples, the long-term (!) and often complicated right to maintain two jobs not synonymous with or a guarantee for the realization of dual careers. Because of that Couples would do well not to have any gainful employment with the achievement equate to a career (cf. also chapter 1 in this A book).

THE END

Description

All in all, fabricating a fruitful vocation is certainly not a simple accomplishment, however it is conceivable when you have the right outlook, abilities, and demeanor. Recollect that achievement isn't just about accomplishing your objectives yet additionally about keeping a balance between serious and fun activities, supporting connections, and adding to the general public. Your profession process might be loaded up with promising and less promising times, however it is vital to remain versatile, adaptable, and ready to gain from your slip-ups. At last, making a profession together is tied in with making a satisfying life for you and everyone around you. Best of luck on your excursion!